outdoor
decorating

project and idea book

julie taylor/sandra salamony/maryellen driscoll/nora richter greer

First published in the United States of America by

Rockport Publishers, Inc.

33 Commercial Street

Gloucester, Massachusetts 01930-5089

Telephone: (978) 282-9590

Fax: (978) 283-2742

www.rockpub.com

Library of Congress Cataloging-in-Publication Data available

ISBN 1-59253-046-X

10 9 8 7 6 5 4 3 2 1

Cover Image: Front cover: Grey Crawford/Lise Claiborne Matthews, AIA, ASID (top); Carlos Domenech/Marco Guinaldo Design (bottom left); Bobbie Bush Photographer/www.bobbiebush.com (bottom middle); Tim Street-Porter/Mark Mack (bottom right)

Back cover: Brian Vanden Brink

Grateful acknowledgment is given to Sandra Salamony and Maryellen Driscoll for their work from *A Gardener's Craft Companion* on pages 183–297; to Nora Richter Greer and A. Bronwyn Llewellyn for their work from *Outdoor Decorating and Style Guide* on pages 6–23, 34–35, 78–79, 116–117, 146–147, 154–155, 180–181; and to Julie D. Taylor for her work from *Outdoor Rooms* on pages 24–33, 36–77, 80–115 118–145, 148–153, 156–179.

Printed in China

Maryellen Driscoll, a tireless writer, crafter, gardener, and cook, lives on a small working farm at the foot of the Adirondack Mountains. A former editor at *Cook's Illustrated*, she is author of *The Paper Shade Book* and *Gardener's Craft Companion* and has contributed to several national magazines and major newspapers.

Nora Richter Greer is an architecture and design critic, whose professional writing career began in 1977 at *Architecture* magazine. Since then she has written for numerous magazines and newspapers, as well as contributed to and authored more than a dozen books on architecture, urban design, and interior design. With advance degrees in journalism and creative writing, Ms. Greer resides in Washington, D.C.

Julie D. Taylor sees herself as a "design evangelist," whose passions include architecture, interior design and furnishings, landscape architecture, and graphic design. A former magazine editor, she is principal and founder of Taylor & Company in Beverly Hills, California, which provides marketing, public relations, and communications services to professionals, manufacturers, institutions, and organizations involved in the fields of architecture, design, and furnishings. She holds a Bachelor of Arts degree in Art History from Northwestern University, and is an exhibited artist and published photographer.

Influenced by her master gardener father and decorator mother, **Sandra Salamony** is especially gifted at combining botanicals with nontraditional crafting techniques. Most recently the author of *Hand Lettering for Crafts*, she has also collaborated with Mary Ann Hall on *The Crafter's Project Book*, both published by Rockport Publishers. Her craft designs have appeared in many books and magazines.

contents

introduction

Unless you live in southern California or the French Riviera—where the weather is perfect all year long—most people eagerly await the arrival of spring and summer. We all dream of sitting outdoors on a warm night, sipping a cool drink and staring up at the stars. The idea is a romantic one, but unless you have put some thought into your outdoor space, the reality is often not quite as pleasurable as the mid-winter dream makes it seem.

As with indoor spaces, outdoor spaces need to be planned and decorated to reflect your style. Like any interior room of the house, you need to think through how the space will be used before decorating; otherwise you'll be continually frustrated with its lack of purpose.

Outdoor decorating is just an extension of your indoor space and your personal style. *Outdoor Decorating: A Project and Idea Book* provides you with all the know-how and inspiration you will need to make your outdoor space both stylish and practical. Packed with planning and style advice and techniques and instructions to use elements taken from nature to create your own outdoor decorations and art pieces, this book is the definitive outdoor style book and the most comprehensive practical book available on decorating outdoor space.

DESIGN
BASICS

GETTING STARTED

Take a radical step today and look at your outdoor space with new eyes. Pull your favorite chair out onto the lawn, terrace, patio, or balcony. Remove everything else. (Or if you can't clear away heavy objects, pretend you have a clean slate.) Be patient. Observe the space at different times of the day. Imagine the activities you see taking place there—dinner with family or friends, a small cocktail party on a warm summer evening, quiet relaxation with a book. Start building the perimeters of the room; then add furniture piece by piece. Coordinate what other elements you may want, working down to specific, minute decorative accents. Think three-dimensionally. Consider the shifting outdoor environment and, ultimately, the rotating seasons. Your outdoor room should provide a rich tapestry of color and texture, light and shade, which fluctuates with the time of day and season of the year and is always a refreshing enclave of fresh air, changing winds and temperatures, and natural sights and sounds.

Not everyone will begin with a clean slate with every outdoor project. But it's a useful exercise to consider even when just redecorating. In your mind, clear away the clutter and start afresh. Why not consider, just for the moment, changing the size, shape, or placement of your outdoor room and its contents—or its personality?

The overall goal is to extend indoor living outside in a way that is highly livable—both comfortable and practical—but also lovely. Connect with nature in your own personal way. Create a truly unique place to relax, entertain, eat, or just escape.

SURVEYING THE TURF

To make the most of your outdoor space, you need to undertake two critical tasks. The first is to survey the property, taking stock of its strengths and weaknesses. Secondly, essential questions need to be asked about your own lifestyle, needs, and desires, and how you would like to utilize the space. Only then can you actually start planning the more intricate details that will create the mood and atmosphere of your outdoor room.

In an informal way, you've started the visual survey of the space on the preceding pages. Now it's time to dig a bit deeper and put pencil to paper. Start a preliminary drawing marking

above
Clear the deck (or patio or terrace) and survey your outdoor room. Consider what changes you might like to make. Would you like to enlarge the space? Change the orientation? The materials? Add new furniture?

existing plants and spaces that you would like to retain. Notice sun and shade patterns, and if you can, how these patterns might change through the seasons. Determine which views are significant and if the desired vista is fully visible. Note how the site slopes and how level changes are handled—with stairs or just a sloped hill, for instance. Check for interesting natural features, such as rocks or a pond. You'll need to know the condition of your soil and your climatic requirements for planting purposes.

Also consider how your outdoor space looks from inside. And envision how it might look if redesigned. Then take out your tape measure and try to sketch the site, realizing that in the end, you may seek the help of a professional landscape architect, architect, or horticulturalist, especially if you undertake a complicated renovation.

The goal is to determine the best use for the outdoor space. Typically, you can create several different rooms, unless, of course, your property is constricted on a small urban site. The second task helps you shape those rooms to closely respond to your needs. Question how each is going to be used and by whom. Think about transitions between rooms. Consider movement through the rooms. In the end, the success of the design may depend on how well the room works as much as how good it looks. Keep in mind that your budget concerns may affect your final design choices.

The twenty-one pertinent questions presented here are not inclusive but only meant to start the inquiry. Recognize that each home setting is unique, and of course, the use of an outdoor room depends on preference, but also on climate. Each location brings specific landscaping choices for outdoor rooms and different requirements for treating the natural elements, such as sun, shade, wind, and rain.

twenty-one questions

1. What outdoor space do you now use?
2. Who in your family uses it and for what purposes?
3. How often do you use it?
4. Do you consider it an outdoor room?
5. If you use the space for entertainment, do you find that it large enough for your requirements?
6. Is there is place to barbecue and dine?
7. Do you feel that your outdoor room is otherwise adequate, or could it be put to better use?
8. Are there other spaces that could become outdoor rooms?
9. Do you have easy access to the outdoor room from indoors?
10. Do you want to redesign the room or redecorate or both?
11. How much of the hardscape needs improvement—i.e., the paving, walkways, fences?
12. Is the landscaping in good shape or does it need some refreshing? Do you like to work in the garden?
13. If your room is a porch or gazebo or patio, do the walls or floors need improvement?
14. Do you need to do any electrical work around your outdoor room? Does this need upgrading?
15. How would you like to decorate your outdoor room—in what style: formal, romantic, exotic, minimal, eclectic?
16. Would you like to incorporate some of the elements you have now? What new elements would you like?
17. If you could have ten luxuries, what would they be?
18. Do you have enough privacy?
19. Is your lighting system adequate?
20. What is your budget?
21. What are some compromises to meet that budget?

outdoor rooms

The vocabulary of outdoor rooms is quite extensive and includes the following:

ARBOR: A light, open structure of plants twined together and self-supporting or supported on a light latticework frame.

ARCH: A curved construction spanning an opening.

BALCONY: A protected platform on a building, supported from below, with a railing or balustrade.

BOWER: A sheltered structure in a garden.

CONSERVATORY: A glass-enclosed room for the cultivation and display of plants.

COURTYARD: An open area, partially or fully enclosed by buildings or other walls, adjacent to or within a house.

DECK: A flat, open platform.

ENTRYWAY: An entry passage.

GARDEN ROOM: The room in the house that presents itself to the garden.

GAZEBO: A summerhouse with a view.

LOGGIA: An arcaded or colonnaded porch or gallery attached to a larger structure, open on one or more sides.

ORANGERY: The original term for a conservatory.

PATIO: An outdoor area adjoining or enclosed by the walls or arcades of a house; often paved and shaded.

PERGOLA: A structure consisting of parallel colonnades supporting an open roof of girders and cross rafters.

PLAYHOUSE: A small structure for children's recreation.

PORCH: A structure attached to a building to shelter an entrance or to serve as a semienclosed space; usually roofed and generally open sided or glass enclosed.

POTTING SHED: A shed used for potting plants and other garden-support activities.

ROOFTOP TERRACE: A flat roof or a raised space or platform adjoining a building.

SUMMERHOUSE: A garden house of light airy design used in the summer for protection from the sun.

SUNROOM: A sunny room with a large expanse of glass.

TERRACE: A paved embankment with level top.

VERANDA: A covered porch or balcony, extending along the outside of a building, planned for summer leisure.

WRAPAROUND PORCH: A porch that wraps around two or more sides of a house.

PUTTING IT
ALL TOGETHER

You may well be on your way to realizing your perfect outdoor room. But is there such a place? Probably not. Since the natural outdoor environment is anything but static, we probably wouldn't want perfection anyway. Hopefully, though, you may have gleaned some of the nuances necessary to put together the near-perfect outdoor room and with that new knowledge, more enthusiastically delve into the planning process. You'll discover many surprises along the way. In the end, you'll enjoy hours relaxing and entertaining in your beautifully designed outdoor room, an environment that will weather well with the passing seasons and the years.

step-by-step formula to outdoor decoration

1. Preliminary review of outdoor space(s)
2. Full examination of needs and potential uses of outdoor room(s)
3. Type of space(s) desired—i.e., type of outdoor room(s)
4. Remodeling or building anew
5. Budget
6. Style options
7. Establishing the room's bones/perimeters
8. Hardscape versus softscape
9. Furniture options
10. Hard materials
    a. Paving
    b. Ceiling
    c. Walls or fencing
11. Fabric and color
12. Decorative accents
13. Special features
14. Maintenance
15. Enjoyment, relaxation, entertainment

left
All the essential elements come together in a lavish loggia/pool pavilion. The blue cushions and the teak and wicker chaise lounges reflect the color of the sky and water. A sense of proportion and balance is achieved in the arrangement, and a bit of whimsy, with the alligator sculpture sitting at the near end of the pool.

ESTABLISHING BOUNDARIES

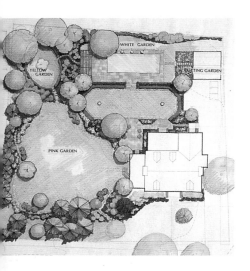

Establishing the boundaries of an outdoor room can be a daunting task. After all, we're accustomed to having the strict dimensions of our interior rooms preordained. Obviously, the dimensions of an attached front, wraparound, or side porch will already be set (unless you are adding on to your home). Designing these outdoor rooms will prove much more familiar to you than laying out a new patio or building a deck. For the latter you will need to have a keen sense of capacity from the beginning: How much and what size furniture will be there, and what other accessories, such as a barbeque or a fountain will be incorporated? How many people will the space accommodate? Building a deck to hold six is different from building a deck that can easily handle a party of fifty. Think about moving freely around the outdoor room, especially when it is decorated with furniture. Outdoor furniture can be a bit bulky, so take that into consideration. Draw plans with cutouts for the furniture, or use three-dimensional objects, such as cardboard boxes, to test your space planning.

Except for, perhaps, apartment and condominium living, most home sites offer the possibility of several outdoor rooms. These can usually be connected by pathways through gardened areas or can actually be one contiguous space, broken into separate areas. Think of creating focal points, as you would indoors, gathering places where people can congregate and provide an easy flow between the various "rooms." Room divisions are naturally created if the property slopes or changes levels and the shifts in grade are emphasized. Consider different personalities or styles for the various rooms.

room/shape perceptions

- A square room draws attention to each corner, which in an outdoor room provides a somewhat rigid construction.

- In comparison, a circle stretches outward and creates a nonrestricted feeling.

- Breaking a space into different rooms can either make a small space seem larger or a large space seem more intimate.

- Rooms can be divided by planting, trellises, fences, hedging, or shifts in levels.

- Brickwork laid widthways across a narrow paved room will widen the space and laid lengthways, will elongate a room.

- Often a room will take an organic shape dictated by the preexisting contours or features, such as a meandering stream, a path, or a coastline.

basic design concepts

Outdoor rooms can assume many forms—porches, patios, terraces, gazebos, etc. (as discussed previously). When designing an outdoor room, start as you would an interior space, with the structural foundation or the "bones" of the room. Examine the given—the walls, floor, and ceiling that exist, even if the ceiling is the sky! Consider changing the proportions and lines of the room. This is a simple, fundamental concept, but only if you think of the space as three-dimensional can you apply the basic principles of design, such as proportion, scale, balance, rhythm, and repetition. These, in turn, will produce a harmonious outdoor room—or if you like, one with a sense of discord, but planned dissonance.

proportion, balance, and scale

We seek a sense of balance and proportion for visual comfort. If that balance is missing on purpose, a designer can be making an explicit eclectic statement, intentionally drawing the viewer's eye to specific objects. More often than not, though, we're looking for a balance between the sizes of objects. So carefully select your decorative elements. Since we're looking for a balance between solids and voids, you need to think of your space in three-dimensional terms. If the elements in your outdoor room vary widely in scale, try grouping smaller pieces together to counterbalance one larger piece. Use landscaping and potted plants as balancing objects. Also try to think of the pieces of furniture as objects of sculpture. In that way, you'll focus on the particulars of a chair or table and make a conscious effort to seek good design. It's best not to overload your space with too many objects. You can always keep a supply of portable chairs nearby, for easy use when necessary.

It's often useful to use the grid of the house to help establish the layout proportions for an outdoor room. For example, if the façade of the house breaks equally into four windows, the distances between each could set the lines of your planning grid. Extend this grid out from the walls of the house and visually plan your outdoor room.

As outdoor rooms relate so closely to nature, often they take on organic shapes, so another visual clue can be an organic shape found in nature, such as the path of the brook in your backyard. Or sometimes the contours are simply modeled on a relaxed, flowing organic form. Often the shapes are repeating and even overlapping.

nature's framework

A huge range of plants is available commercially for gardeners. We usually consider them by commonly known categories such as trees, shrubs, bulbs, annuals, perennials, grasses, etc. For your outdoor room, plants may just be a decorative element, or foliage may provide structure or part of the framework for your space. If building a framework of plants, it's useful to consider categories established by the renowned British landscape designer John Brookes. He considers these the three-dimensional shapes of the horticulturalist's framework:

■ The specials: the star performers that form focal points; a plant with a distinctive quality that allows it to stand out as a sculptural feature.

■ The skeletons: the green background that will ensure year-round enclosure, provide a windscreen, and generally mold the garden space, or the bones, of a framework.

■ The decoratives: the plants to be displayed in front of the skeleton.

■ The pretties: the perennials for flower and foliage interest in spring and summer.

■ The infill plantings: the transitory splashes of color as the seasons change and the invaluable gap fillers.

left
Exotic plants form a framework and act as focal points in this aquatic outdoor room. The red cushion adds more heat to the tropical climate.

far left
The view down this loggia shows a world in balance. The overall architecture, with its columns and arches, provides a consistent superstructure under which are placed groupings of wicker chairs and metal tables.

rhythm, repetition, and unity

When the design of a room—interior or exterior—seems visually pleasing it generates a sense of unity. Each element is strong in itself but together, they flow into a delightful three-dimensional composition. Tools to reach this unity are repetition and rhythm. Expert gardeners repeat certain plant colors, textures, and species throughout a garden to bring rhythm and unity. The same can be done with other decorative elements. Actually, when a certain style is chosen—say classical—some repetition is automatically built in. Most likely, you will choose a set of matching cast iron chairs to go with the glass-covered, cast iron table. The classical columns of the porch may be echoed in the side table pediment. What about adding a cast iron lounge rather than turning to teak? Your

pots may be pewter-colored rather than clay to continue the cool tonality.

In a more relaxed environment, repeat other materials or shapes, such as brick, wood, or fencing materials. Or develop an alternating pattern between two or more materials, which provides a sense of unity, in the paving, for instance. These contrasts can work, too, as long as there is an underlying sense of proportion and the effect is strong enough to provide real visual excitement.

If mixing styles is a preference, go for the eclectic look, but do so with some planned order or rhythm to your choices. Overall, strive for simplicity, for the understated is often more elegant than the overstated and cluttered.

right
Tucked beneath a rustic shelter is a casual daybed; its bulky horizontal shape is balanced by three square peephole windows set vertical in the wall above. Additionally, the bed is flanked by a rustic chair on one end and a collection of large pots on the other.

color promotes unity

Color can be the rhythm and repetition that establishes unity. The azure blue floor tiles of the terrace near the pool, for example, are echoed in the blue and white cushions that are reflected in the blue sky and the blue flowers in the vase on the glass table. That may be enough to hold the composition together.

Depending on location, colors used in outdoor rooms don't necessarily need to be flamboyant, but can, perhaps, be most pleasant when melding into the natural environment. Tans, grays, browns, greens, and the color of brick sit comfortably against outdoor materials. Remember, too, that nature's colors will change dramatically from one season to the next.

focal points and pathways

When arranging the furniture and objects in your outdoor room, it's useful to establish a focal point, a place where the human eye can focus and rest. For example, when guests enter, what do they focus on? The table set festively for dinner? A decorative swatch of fabric hung on the porch wall? A garden sculpture lit dramatically at night? A collection of exotic plants set in a group of container pots in the corner of the patio? Or the brightly-colored pillows arranged on your white wicker settee? Try organizing the rest of the outdoor room as a more tranquil three-dimensional composition around the chosen focal point.

Make sure there is easy access into and through the space. The entrances in and out should be clearly discernable. The flow through should be as smooth as it is in an indoor room. The issue of movement in an outdoor space clearly illustrates how important the planning process is— that one needs to keep in mind the rather bulky size of outdoor furniture and also how many people you expect the room to accommodate, at the maximum.

The pathways to your outdoor room are an important part of the design as they set the mood. Paths should be of a material that is compatible in color, texture, and mood with the outdoor room, but not necessarily identical. Entryways can merely hint at what is to be expected in the outdoor room.

For practical purposes, width should never be less than 3 feet. To gain a sense of unity, relate the lines of a path to the width of the existing doors or windows of the house. The path's shape—whether straight or curved—and the length will obviously depend on each individual design, but, again, the pathway's design should reinforce and introduce the overall theme of the outdoor room, or act as a transition from one room to another, by combining several materials.

right
Step out the French doors and up the stairs to the garden. The stone stairs complement the stone base of the conservatory and provide a gentle transition to the lush greenery. Potted plants add decoration.

steps and stairways: quick tips

Steps become an architectural feature when used to bridge dramatic changes in level. A gradual, slight and broad change in level can be used as a device to create separate rooms. When designing steps and stairways consider the following:

- Outdoor steps usually need a greater scale than indoor ones. In other words, you can be more generous with the design of outdoor steps.

- Generally, the higher each step is, the faster one goes up. Use steep steps to move up and down faster. A handrail may be necessary for safety on steep steps.

- Planting material will soften the edges of steep steps.

- The material used often dictates dimensions.

- Place emphasis on the steps leading to the front of the house. Take clues from the material and scale of the house's elevation.

- Different materials can be used for treads and risers. Keep the treads generous (no less than 12 to 14 inches).

- Create generous landings to break up long flights of steps.

- Shallow, slow steps can act as impromptu places to sit and rest—or to place potted plants.

TAKING ADVANTAGE OF VISTAS

A fabulous vista puts a high price on a piece of property. A view out to the blue waters of the ocean or over the surrounding hillsides offers hours of pleasure. Yet, whether the view is quite this fantastic or not, every outdoor room should have a vista. It may be of the weeping cherry tree in one's backyard rather than the sun setting over the sea, yet that view may hold some promise—and be the only vista available. Try to take advantage of it. Rearrange it, if necessary.

First determine if there is a vista that is being obstructed—by overgrown vegetation, particularly—or one that is not in focus. When you discover your vista, orient your outdoor room to frame this view. Think of it as you would a beautiful picture, with the structure of the room being the frame, and examine the opening from many angles. Make sure the edges of the frame please you, or soften the frame with plants

such as ivy. Reveal the whole vista at once, or conceal parts of it to be seen only from certain perspectives. You may actually see too much and may need to add trees or shrubs in the garden to provide a secondary frame of the view.

Or create your own. This will, obviously, take time. You'll need to plant a lovely, decorative tree, or find a dramatic piece of sculpture, or add a bubbling fountain. Or add a gazebo or trellis to the edge of your property. Invite birds, butterflies, or other wildlife onto your property.

Don't let the vista disappear on a moonless night. Throw some spotlights on it, if no other lighting exists, to at least bring some of the ambience alive. You may not be able to capture that distant vista but you may be able to hint at what is there and entice the viewer to come back at daybreak.

birds and butterflies

Invite the presence of wildlife into the boundaries of your outdoor room with a few simple features. A small pond, waterfall, or fountain will attract birds, as will ornamental birdbaths, birdhouses, and/or birdfeeders. Invitations revolve around food. Hummingbirds and butterflies like nectar-producing flowers, such as lantana, impatiens, and zinnias. Hummingbirds also prefer red, pink, and orange flowers. Larger birds desire plants with winter berries, fruits, and seed heads, such as crabapple, dogwood, elaeagnus, and firethorn. An inch-deep container of water is best for birds and butterflies. Keep the water clean. The splashing sound of water will attract more birds. Overhanging branches out of reach of cats and dogs provide secure perches for birds.

below
The table is set for dinner for four
at dusk on the balcony terrace, under
the trellis, with a dramatic city view
in the background.

LANDSCAPE—
HARD VERSUS SOFT

Discuss your outdoor room plans with a landscape architect and the terms *hardscape* and *softscape* will come up quickly, unless, perhaps, you are designing a sunroom or conservatory. As the term implies, hardscape includes all the "hard" materials—the paving, wall, and ceiling surfaces, structures, furniture, etc. The softscape is the foliage. Balance between the two is the key objective. Of course, the experts will have their own opinions of what the perfect proportion is. The stonemason will inevitably suggest a larger stone wall than the landscape designer would.

Actually, a large part of the pleasure of having an outdoor room is the connection with nature. So, when choosing your furniture—and the rest of your hardscape—you need to consider the nature—or softscape—around you. Balance the size and bulk of your furniture with the greenery, or at least consider what might grow in your garden. Foliage can provide abundant color, texture, and fragrance. Plants can focus views, provide privacy, cool down hot summer days, shelter from winds, and attract wildlife. Plants grow, bloom, change color, and mature. The garden is never static and can be a source of great pleasure.

Encyclopedias chronicle plant species that are appropriate for specific climatic zones. If you are truly a beginner, it may be useful, however, to simply survey what plants exist on your site and then think about what might make the outdoor room more attractive. Start with deciduous shade trees and work down in size to smaller decorative trees. Evergreens are popular because they maintain their foliage year-round. Shrubs are considered foundation plants since they often define the overall shape and limits of a garden. Roses, of course, are international favorites, and are available in a wide variety of species. Garden beds can be filled with perennials or annuals of an amazing variety. Vines trail over trellises and arches. And grass or other ground plants cover the lawn. Landscape architects strive for color year-round, depending on the climate. There has been great interest lately in planting foliage that is natural to a particular region. The novice gardener might also balk at the idea of tending a large green space, yet planting options exist that are low maintenance. For small terraces and patios, potted plants and flowers can go a long way toward adding some natural greenery. Consult your local nursery. Even well-trained gardeners may wish to consult their local nursery!

LANDSCAPE STYLE

Decorating styles can define the appearance of our outdoor rooms. You can, for instance, choose among the historical styles, such as the classical, De Stijl, Edwardian, Greek revival, International Style, Queen Anne, Renaissance, or Victorian, among many others. Or you can consider style in a less formal interpretation, such as modern, romantic, exotic, rustic, urbane, or eclectic. Perhaps, the strictly historical is easiest to define. Other characterizations become less surefooted and, in fact, often reflect the personality of the viewer and the design viewed—there may be several different interpretations for the same design.

And what does it mean to possess a sense of style? How do you know that the juxtapositions of materials and shapes, and colors produce a delightful arrangement? In other words, can one learn to be a pleasing stylist?

The sampling of styles here and in later chapters of *Outdoor Decorating* is meant to be provocative, not definitive. The best way to determine what style appeals most to you and how to style your outdoor room is to survey as many outdoor spaces as possible. And experiment. You can't ignore location, climate, setting, and the surrounding architecture. You can embellish what you have in any way that you like. Remember, though, that elegance often comes from simplicity—or at least a balance of elements.

above
Rustic: Relax in luxury in the open air, while living the rustic, laid-back life. Under a rustic wood shelter, place a throw rug over brick floor to match the red leather sofa, covered with Indian print cushions. Rustic but chic.

OUTSIDE IN

From the *trompe l'oeil* wall paintings of far-away vistas found in ancient Pompeii to Philip Johnson's Glass House, where hardly a mullion blocks the view of his Connecticut estate, people have hungered for a feeling of the outdoors in their protected, interior living spaces. As homeowners become more involved in their garden spaces and live outdoors more, they also want their indoor spaces to be veritable windows on their world.

Traditionally, these indoor/outdoor spaces are breakfast rooms and porch sitting areas. We'll see, however, that the rest of the house can enjoy these spaces in the form of all-glass areas, with light and nature invited into living rooms, bedrooms, and bathrooms.

◄ ► These two sunrooms form just part of the indoor/outdoor areas of a house in the exclusive and beautiful area of Broad Beach in southern California. Angular bay windows allow ocean views and let the light in, setting the stage for the plush and comfort of deep-pile upholstery and leather furniture in the interiors. Angular bay windows are used again in the upper-level master bedroom. Both sunrooms afford visual access to the terraces beyond.

GLASS HOUSES

There are many advantages to living in an all-glass room (never mind that maxim about not throwing stones!). Light and views are allowed in, while harsh elements are kept out. Vast expanses of glass have connoted closeness to nature and spirit since the Gothic cathedrals were built.

▶ ▶ Situating their house around a courtyard, the architects create an open home that stresses the connections between the indoors and out through light, volume, and materials. The long great room is flanked by full-height windows looking into the interior courtyard and half-height windows facing a skyline of tall trees. Concrete interior flooring flows out to the courtyard with only the glass sliding doors to separate the inside from the outside. The interior wood ceiling corresponds to the exterior wood detailing. The loft-like feeling of the great room is amplified by varying levels of windows that face views on all sides of the courtyard, neighboring park land, and San Francisco Bay.

Formal and informal dining spaces are separated by a feature wall in this house situated on a bluff overlooking the beach. The breakfast room sits in one of the several pavilion-like spaces that radiate from the central circulation spine of the house. The freestanding divider wall separates the breakfast room from the dining room, while maintaining a sense of openness in the space. On the breakfast room side, the glass-tiled wall has functional storage space, while serving as an artistic background for the dining room.

Stunning and brave in its starkness and complexity, this house gives extreme attention to the glass-enclosed court and lap pool. The two-story glass-fronted court acts as a protective field for the more private living and bedroom spaces. Reaching 250 feet (75 meters) out into the landscape, the glass-and-wood enclosed lap pool is a bridge to the outdoors.

▶▶ A second-floor den is seemingly suspended within this dramatic house. The curved window-wall is delineated with wood and equipped with two operable windows. Inside, the wood-paned window wall is juxtaposed with seamless glass, which opens the space to the view below, as does the glass floor panel with view of the pool.

Located in the remains of an old barn foundation on a Pennsylvania farm, this house accommodates the client's wishes for openness and privacy, as well as for rooms defined by mood and atmosphere. Planes of glass and stone work together with walls meandering in service to views and light. The contrast between ancient stone and modern glass creates a mood of both tension and intrigue.

▲ This house stresses verticality in its attempt to take up as little space as possible in its natural surroundings. The dramatic entry room rises three stories, with a sitting area on the first floor, and variations on visual access on the upper floors. Views looking out are of a mature deciduous forest and Maryland's Severn River.

◀ ▲ Clever use of space allows for a greenhouse in the addition to this 160-year-old home in New England. The glass-block upper-level deck is the ceiling for the lower-level greenhouse. Additional windows are installed for greater light, while the room is bolstered by a variety of stone textures.

This beach house extends outdoor living to even the most private pleasures of the bath, which is given a spectacular view of the ocean, while protected behind glass. An outdoor spa is complete with fireplace, roof covering, and plantings for privacy and warmth.

Determined to create a home with a connection to the outdoors, the architects and client visited Japan to observe how buildings relate to gardens. Bedrooms and other private spaces open up to an interior courtyard, while main living spaces are encased in glass, wood, and copper pavilion-like structures. One side opens to a gravel courtyard, while the other looks upon a lush, natural garden.

outdoor easy — bringing natural light in

Bringing the outdoors in involves structural changes to your house, unless you already have a sunroom or a porch. In northern climates, a southern orientation is preferred, and in southern climates, a northern one. The ideal construction should utilize as much glazing as possible, with the opportunity to open the windows to the fresh air. Through the glass, the incoming sun will provide healthy natural light, as well as outgoing views into the garden, which can provide a calming connection to nature. Even if the sun isn't shining or there are overhead shade trees, solar heat will be transferred into the room.

Choose flooring accordingly, for solar heat can be stored and released in the evening. In some cases, designers will make special efforts to harness this solar energy. Additionally, skylights are an excellent device for opening a room to light and can be placed deep within a house. Or try a cathedral ceiling, placing glass in the eaves and opening up the entire room to natural daylight.

Many types and styles of insulated windows are available. Manufacturers offer windows in all shapes and sizes and also windows that are designed to specifically deter solar heat gain. Attractive systems of blinds, shades, and curtains also help. Try blinds that automatically open and close, depending on the time of day or the orientation of the sun.

If tearing down the walls of the house isn't an option, there are less costly ways to brighten an interior room—to make it feel like a sunroom. Take down the heavy curtains or blinds and replace them with shear window coverings to allow as much natural light as possible to enter. Strategically hang a large, decorative mirror on a wall to reflect that natural light around the room. Or hang a couple of mirrors that can bounce light back and forth. Paint the room a bright, light color that reflects the sun. White or off-white is an obvious choice, but even consider yellow. Bright yellows make a room appear lighter by simulating sunlight. And, depending on the yellow, it can make a very large room feel cozier. Yellow is best where more energy is desired, as well as to provide a cheerful atmosphere.

right
Add a light, airy sunroom to the perimeter of your house. Special solar glass, as well as a ceiling fan, can help reduce heat gain. This cheerful, sunny room is an attraction in the gloomy winter.

PROTECTED PORCHES

Extending from the house, yet still encased in some sort of wall, the protected porch may be bolstered by glass, shutters, or screens. The screen affords numerous possibilities and freedom to homeowners who desire the gentle breezes and fragrances of the outdoors, but want to avoid strong winds, rain, and local fauna (bugs!).

◄ ► The legendary Los Angeles design icon Tony Duquette dedicated his 175-acre (70-hectare) ranch in Malibu to wondrous enchantment. The designer clearly creates a greenhouse-like space with potted plants, exotic sculptures, and island-inspired furniture. The lavish sensuality harks back to Duquette's roots in Hollywood, where he designed many sets and costumes, and counted Mary Pickford and David O. Selznick among his clients. Like Eden past, this enchanted place is no more, having burned to the ground in one of the many wildfires that plague the beauty of Malibu.

▲ ▲ Allowing airflow into the home, this semicircular porch is also a quiet area for reflection onto the open pasture beyond. The arcing room plays along with the geometric forms of the house—stucco-clad volumes topped with metal roofs.

The sidewalk-like path winds its way from standard-issue chain link fencing through the perfectly sewn lawn, to an abbreviated picket fence, ending at a screened-in porch with a countrified pediment entrance. The porch not only augments the existing house, but, in fact, defines it visually.

A series of arbors alternates between open areas and screened-in porches, such as this one on a Texas ranch. Brick brings a slightly more refined ground element than the natural ground cover outside, and hand-crafted furniture adds curved elements to the angularity of the space.

▲ Three barn-like basilica structures
in varying stages of transparency—
an open steel-grid structure, one in
stone and screen, and a galvanized-
metal cladded volume—define a
home that celebrates industrial
architecture. Bounded by horizontal
screen bands, a large open space
serves as a dramatic dining room.

The architect furthers exploration of the vernacular, wood-frame designs found at the Seaside community of Florida by using elements of transparency and exaggeration. An upper-level "shutter room," designated as a secondary living space, uses floor-to-ceiling red shutters to create a private hideaway. Like the rest of the house, it is screened by contemporary lattice work that heightens the skeletal, architectural quality of the design.

OPEN DOORS

Open the door and let all of the outdoors in. That's the thought behind these rooms, where doors and windows are unified, and the line between interior and exterior is forever blurred.

▲ Charged with creating "an old Eastern verandah" from a former recording studio, the designer uses a mix of furnishings to create space for relaxation and entertainment. Garden ornaments and topiaries mix with Neo-Classical elements for a formal, yet comfortable, space.

Situated in a California national forest, this weekend retreat may commonly see at least two feet (.6 meters) of winter snow. To take full advantage of the spring and summer temperatures, the architects installed glass garage doors that can be fully opened. The house is designed with the living areas on the upper level for full views of mountains and valley. Decks emerge from either side of the living room, adding further emphasis to the seamless space.

► ► The architect's own home embodies southern California living and style in its insistence on equal outdoor and indoor spaces, as well as in the combination of industrial and natural materials. In the dual dining rooms, park-like outdoor furniture rests on both floors, whether they be burnished concrete or decking constructed from recycled wood forms. A translucent scrim adds privacy.

▲ A gentle symmetry gives this seating area a serene feeling, along with the bright-white window panes, sculptural lamp, and upholstered furniture. The plan for this Long Island, New York, renovation is to integrate architecture, garden, water, and interior.

▲ Nearly floor-to-ceiling glass on three sides creates a complete feeling of openness. Sliding doors lead out to a grand patio facing Florida's Intracoastal Waterway. Overscale wicker seating is upholstered in neutral colors for a light, beach-house feeling.

Dating from the 1920s, this historic Connecticut home is given a sunroom with pale green–paned, articulated window walls. Outdoor paving material is brought indoors to connect the room to the natural site.

▲ A true indoor/outdoor feeling is achieved by the tile flooring, teak furniture, and overhead fans. Varying-height doors and sidelights let in soft light from outdoors. Set for dining and relaxing, this space evokes further serenity in its monochrome tones taken from the natural teak and sisal.

▲ Reality and illusion are at play in this octagonal breakfast room, where the designer installs French doors for physical access to the garden, along with decorative painting for more spiritual access. Other elements that bring the garden inside include wicker-and-iron furniture and an antique garden light fixture.

HANGING ON

According to the humorous social critic Fran Lebowitz, "the outdoors is what you must pass through in order to get from your apartment into a taxicab." For homeowners today, the spaces between two forms of shelter are more than incidental atmosphere. These spaces that "hang on" to the house are celebrated and doted on. They connote leisure, luxury, and beauty. They embody our ability to tame and enjoy nature at the same time. Here, we'll look at spaces that are structurally connected to the house, yet fully intended as outdoor rooms. Porches and entries, patios and terraces, decks and balconies, and rooftops—whether in a large country manse, or a small city apartment—are vital living spaces for casual entertaining, family leisure time, or a personal respite from a busy day.

◀ ▶ This isolated ridge-top house features a wrap-around porch with entertainment area leading from the interior living room to the pool. Exposed wood trusses and cedar siding connect the inside and outside areas of the house. The cathedral-like archway artfully frames mountain views, further reinforcing the house's relationship to its natural surroundings and the architects' concentration on edges and openings.

PORCHES AND ENTRIES

How you feel when you walk into your home—or how you greet guests—is a driving force behind creating pleasant, welcoming spaces for the front porch and entryway. By definition, a porch is a covered front entry, yet the form is used, of course, on all sides of a home.

▶ Turning an uninteresting, 1960s "developer special" into a traditional home more suited to its New England surroundings, the architect includes this farmhouse porch for authenticity. Traditional clapboard siding, bay windows, Colonial detailing, and contrasting trim bring the house back to the historic roots of the area. Contemporary touches, such as the open ceiling area of the porch, bring the house into today.

▲ ▶ Drama, light, and space combine
in the central porch for a large
Florida home. The architect
combines Classicism and
Modernism in the spare capitals
and symmetric design. Asian-
influenced furniture and objects
create a sophisticated space for
lounging and viewing the pool and
the Intracoastal Waterway beyond.

▶ ▶ With elements of Mediterranean and Classicism, this back porch area for the architect's own home remains clean and simple. Additional architectural elements, such as the dramatic Douglas-fir roof and Spanish tile, contribute rustic interest to the porch area, which overlooks backyard and guest house. Teak furniture in comfortable proportions makes this an alternate family living room.

▶ A drab screened-in porch is transformed into a lush garden platform, complete with tiled pond. The tile, in colors of the Mediterranean, corresponds to the feeling of the house and accents the natural colors of the plants. A stone path leads from the terrace to an outdoor seating area with a panoramic view of the garden.

▶ The deep porch off the kitchen is a bright, sunny area for dining or lounging. The architect brings warmth to the stark opening with cheerful, oversize furniture, which he designed and painted yellow.

▲ This house on Narragansett Bay in Rhode Island is sited specifically to take full advantage of the sweeping view. The broad porch is accessed from living room, dining room, kitchen, and den, emphasizing the homeowners' wishes for waterside entertaining and living spaces.

▶ All the comforts of indoors are re-created in this covered porch nook, complete with fireplace and area rug. The owners, fond of the California wine country, but living in Beverly Hills, wanted rustic elements of log beams and Mediterranean tile roofing added to their otherwise Modern house.

▲ Bold composition and saturated
colors recall the work of Mexican
architect Luis Barragàn. Copper
cladding and irregularly cut stone
add to the rich colorations for the
entry, which sports two lounge
chairs for a quick respite.

► The porch of this showcase house is transformed into an informal study. Furniture and accessories recall world travels, while fringed exterior drapes add an element of fancy and luxury.

◄ The architects use their own home as a continual experimentation ground to try out new ideas in outdoor living. Heightening the Mediterranean style of the house are iron accessories, ethnic furniture, and tiles—cracked and whole—embellishing tables, fireplace, and flooring.

◄ An entry courtyard is created as a transition space between the home and the street for this beachfront property. Frosted panels and French limestone complement the stark whiteness of the architecture, and a high canopy shades the area. Cushioned banquette seating adds softness and counterpoint to the dramatic lines of the furniture.

◄ Extending from the indoor family room is a casual dining area that mixes materials of limestone, marble, steel, and aluminum. Orange trees are encased in a limestone planter-cum-fountain.

► This Mexican outdoor living room is covered by a large thatched palapa roof, which is supported by vine-entwined palm trunks. Fiery colors and rustic furniture add to the minimal space.

▼ A hidden back porch off the library and living room is the perfect spot for a quiet room. Sisal rug softens the outdoor paving. Wicker furniture gives a comfortable, lived-in feeling.

A cozy side porch is outfitted for a Victorian tea with Nantucket-style white wicker furniture and feminine china and table accessories. Picket fence, lattice work, and plenty of climbing vines complete the charming scene.

Recalling the white walls of the Grecian isles, but having a definitely indigenous Mexican palette, this sleeping porch combines all the best motifs of coastal living. Rich Mexican hues and rough timber contrast to the delicately realized pebble sun-ray detailing on the deck.

◄ ▲ Remodeled for a work-at-home
couple with different design
wishes, this split-personality house
gracefully accommodates both.
She wanted a New England
cottage feeling, which is expressed
in the wide porch, shiplap siding,
and traditional details. His office
and outdoor space are much more
contemporary, designed with a
16-foot (5-meter) curved stucco
wall and minimal wood door
frames.

◄ ▼ A variety of porch and terrace spaces create intrigue for a 6,000-square-foot (2,000-square-meter) desert manse. Natural rock outcroppings tie the home to the land, as do the shallow horizontal steps leading to shoji-screen–like doors. Beyond the screens is a private entry court that doubles as a sculpture gallery. The poolside terrace echoes the rock-and-step patterns of the front entrance.

▲ Mexico inspired these English
clothing designers to use their
house as a canvas for a palette of
exciting colors and patterns.
Blues, greens, and reds are
sponged on and wiped off, then
further worked for a weathered,
distressed look. Furniture receives
the same treatment.

◀ ◀ Wicker seating gives a comfortable feeling to this lush porch, over which a long roof is supported by an enormous solid-wood beam from Mexico. Several distinct outdoor spaces serve different functions for the homeowners: protected lounging under the roof, spacious cooking in the open, and shaded dining on the promontory of the hillside. Slate decking is used inside the house and out, as well as along the barbecue buffet.

PATIOS AND TERRACES

Filled with furniture or kept minimal with expert handling of space, patios and terraces are important places for entertaining and recreation. Different paving material—slate, brick, concrete, wood—can change the mood and use of the space from formal and stark to casual and rustic.

▶ ▶ ▶ Serene and sculptural, this house for actor Ricardo Montalban is located in Hollywood but is meant to evoke Mexico. Rough plaster, vibrant colors, and sitting areas in shade and sun fulfill the requirements for both large- and small-scale entertaining. Near the dramatic and cooling pools, deep eaves create a sheltered space for concrete table and chairs (softened by cushions and pillows). Within this house, the architect is continually playing with notions of protection and exposure. A broad, bright terrace boldly faces the city of Los Angeles with its rough, ochre-colored plaster, Mexican tile floor, and cactus plantings that defy the elements.

▲ A sheltered pool and extensive outdoor entertaining area are highlighted by the architect's customary rough-plaster finishes and brilliant colors. The contrast between indoor and outdoor is further heightened in this desert home by areas of deep shade and bright sunlight. The building itself is designed to blend into the landscape, as a simple wall on the crest of a hill.

▼ ▶ Living room, dining room, kitchen, and sitting area are all accommodated on the expansive terrace of this beachfront property. Concrete pavers separate the house from the sand and echo the dominant material used in constructing the terrace. Glass panels protect the owners from the elements while maintaining the transparency that is so important in this home. A curved upper deck is cantilevered over the sitting area, providing shade for the area below as well as additional outdoor space for the private family areas on the second floor. The unique surfacing of the deck comprises metal grating with glass overlay.

▲ The noted Japanese architect Arata Isozaki creates an outdoor gallery for a house and studio, just one block from the California beach. Visitors pass through the broad expanse of concrete to enter this skylit house for an art collector, who uses the terrace as a year-round dining room. A water sculpture and lush environmental art combine with cactus and concrete in a dual comparison of water and land.

◀ ▼ Flexible use of space—and low-cost living—were the ideas behind the original architecture for this 1948 house by California Modernist Gregory Ain. The current architect/homeowner updates the space with a primary-color palette, partially covered terrace, and three distinct garden areas within a small outdoor plot. Easy-to-maintain materials include redwood decking, Arizona red sandstone pavers, and custom-colored concrete.

◄ A 2,000-square-foot (180-square-meter) terrace radiates from the interior breakfast area, kitchen, and family room, creating corresponding areas outdoors. Teak furniture with neutral upholstery blend with the house's concrete-and-wood color scheme.

▶ A fabric canopy shades one seating area on this pool patio, while another area is defined by a glass-block niche. Plays of transparency abound in use of glass block, glazed and unglazed openings, and scrims.

▼ Dealing with a narrow lot and high-rise neighboring buildings, the architect opts for a central courtyard with dining and spa areas. The kitchen opens out to the green Vermont slate paving, which adds to other weatherproof materials, such as water-sealed fir, resin-finished marine plywood, and stucco, to withstand the ocean air.

Perched on a sloping site, this Los Angeles home artfully accommodates space in its planning and design. The pool is protected by the upper level of the house, which is cut with skylight openings. Because it's tucked farther in, the seating area can be given indoor finishes of wood and metal, and accessories such as area rugs. A built-in bench/bar at the end of the pool adds a rich wood tone to the play of subtle light and coloring in this space.

outdoor easy — lighting at night

Nighttime brings out the most romantic in all of us. In outdoor rooms, most anything goes. The moon and stars are nature's built-in illumination. Their faraway brilliance seldom meets our outdoor room needs, and both artificial and candlelight add to the romantic ambience. Typically, candlelight and low-voltage artificial light can soften the most hard-edged spaces and go a long way to meet your lighting needs. But don't be afraid to try different lighting schemes. Obviously, different functions will call for different light intensities, and it's easy to switch lighting levels. In fact, lighting is one of the most versatile design elements.

A great variety of garden lighting is available, including solar-powered lights. Consider spotlighting particular sections of the landscaping for special effect, such as a specific tree or a potted plant. Or try hanging elaborate chandeliers over terraces or on porches. Bring out your antique lamps with wicker or silk shades and blur the boundaries between inside and out. All kinds of lanterns can add festivity or an exotic mood to the scene— Japanese, Scandinavian modern, Greek fisherman, or Moroccan. Or place Deco torchières strategically around the garden and let the glow of their lights soften the darkness. Hurricane lamps do well in windy conditions.

Decorative lighting can also be used to emphasize form, pattern, texture, and shadow; provide general lighting; way finding; and festive sparkles. Like everything else in your outdoor room, it's helpful to plan early for what your lighting needs will be, particularly when your plans involve access to electricity. Most often outdoor lighting will be low-voltage, which involves the use of transformers that reduce the household current to 12 volts. This consumes less energy and is easier to install than standard fixtures, and is safer and more portable. The number of lamps that can be attached is limited. Make sure you choose high-quality metal or plastics. Transformers, cables, and lamps can be hidden in foliage. Use spotlight to uplight or sidelight trees or potted plants, for effect. Another option does exist, however, go entirely solar-powered and supplement that light with candles and torches.

Outdoor lighting has a practical, as well as mood-setting purpose. Visitors need to be safely guided along a path, and perimeter lighting can discourage intruders. It's also easier to barbeque in adequate light. Decorative lighting can be fixed to the house on a porch or deck. Use candles in lanterns or twinkling minilights strung in the trees. Use the lights of the swimming poor for atmosphere. Lighting schemes are easy to change. Next week, try a different lighting combination. It's quite easy to switch torches for candles for twinkle lights. Let your imagination run free.

DECKS AND BALCONIES

Elevated above the ground or cantilevered from the building, decks and balconies provide unique vantage points. Many are used as small meditation spots, with just a simple chair or two, while others are full-scale living and dining rooms.

▶ Decks abound in this architects' house configured around a central courtyard. Keeping with the purity of Modernist design, the deck comprises its essential elements. The space, however, is protected and intimate with the addition of a slatted-wood covering that relates to the shading structures attached to the house itself. Seen from the courtyard below, the deck blends seamlessly into the house's exterior, using the same stone, wood, and metal patterns and materials.

▶ The back deck of a beachfront cottage is nearly one-third of the house's footprint. The open roof mimics the broad overhanging eaves of the main structure and gives partial shade from the Florida sun. Detail in furniture and lighting is kept minimal.

▶ With great architecture to begin with, this 1949 house by Los Angeles Modernist icon Richard Neutra is enhanced by the architect/owner with a galvanized steel container running opposite the low stucco wall to further enclose the private deck. The line between indoor and outdoor disappears when the large sliding-glass doors are opened. The outdoor furniture is also designed by Neutra.

Designed in the tradition of California Modernism, this spectacular house is replete with indoor/outdoor spaces intended for entertainment and casual living. Sliding glass doors allow for a seamless flow between living room and deck. Modernist furniture indoors and outdoors further blurs the distinction between inside and outside.

▲ The architects respond to the site
and natural conditions for this house
on the Connecticut shore. The
upper-level deck is connected to a
covered porch and dining terrace on
lower levels by a single staircase.
Weathered planks and glass blocks
stand up to the elements.

◄ Nestled in a mountain valley, this house was built with the environment in mind, both in its siting and use of materials. Clean architectural lines create a seamless flow between living room and side deck.

► A small bedroom deck overlooks a courtyard space below. Douglas fir, water sealed for protection from the elements, is used for both horizontal and vertical emphasis, as well as for its rich color and contrast to gray stucco.

▼ Serpentine walls echo each others' forms, creating a marble-paved area overlooking a pool below. Indigenous stone from Mallorca, Spain, clads the wall surfaces in a vertical pattern, giving contrast to the broad horizontal geometry.

For their own house, the architects created four separate decks (south, east, west, and roof), each of minimal design, capturing the essence and quiet of simple form. The entry deck is partially covered by one arm of an L-shape, which is the dominant motif in the design of the house. Seemingly piercing the wall, the canopy is clad with corrugated aluminum for the exterior and birch plywood inside.

◀ Spectacular views can be seen from this house with multi-level outdoor rooms, from the pool-side recreation room, to the cantilevered balcony and master suite den. Graphic architectural lines form the triangular balcony spit, which suspends the occupant within the dramatic view.

▶ A small space can reap great rewards with a little attention and strategic choices. A simple, yet effective, sitting area lets the homeowners converse privately, as well as take in the surrounding skyscape. Low-maintenance plants and furniture allow the space to be used year-round with little upkeep and bother.

►► Backed against the forest but facing the ocean, this beach house is used as a company retreat by the firm that built it. Front and back walls of windows afford views from both decks, through the house, and into nature. An expansive back deck runs up against the forest hillside; the smaller front deck overlooks the Oregon coast.

▲ The wonderful climate of Santa Barbara, California, allows this homeowner to use the second-floor balcony as his main dining area. The Spanish Mission flavor of the city is maintained in the distressed beams, terra-cotta flooring, specially made tiles, and iron furniture and lighting fixtures that maintain the style of the 1925 house.

▶ ▶ A glass room opens to the outdoor deck through 9-foot (2.7-meter) doors that provide fine-tuned control over the amount of breeze allowed into the room. Mullions, fretwork, and trellises add elegant strength to the space.

Traditional indoor elements of cushions, fireplace, and sleeping areas are brought outside for the double-level outdoor living space in the architect's own home. The structure is created from Hertz's invention Syndecrete, a synthetic, environmentally friendly concrete-like material. Although hard and industrial gray, the material is softened by 100-percent natural cotton upholstery and wicker seating in the traditional material of rattan. Interior and exterior woodwork in Douglas fir unifies the two spaces.

▼ ▶ A quarter-circle balcony is accessible from a spiral staircase on the outside and from the master suite on the inside. The open space is carved out of a previously closed-in room, with steel beams replacing the torn-down walls. A metal trellis overhead adds to the dynamic geometry of the design.

◄ Beyond the doors, a small deck is cantilevered out from the master bedroom. Concrete walls almost converge in space, but are separated by a glass panel that lets in the pine forest view.

◄ A simple balcony is given dramatic emphasis with the rich colorations and deep tones of the stucco and wood. The shallow eave allows for plays of both brightness and shadow.

▲ A comfortable cottage feeling is achieved with wicker furniture, various floral prints, throw pillows, and white picket railing. Both designer and photographer live in this house, which has several garden spaces.

▲ The designer uses flea-market
finds and old fabrics for a lived-in,
low-maintenance, cozy look for her
own home. This breakfast area is off
the kitchen of a 1940s cottage-style
house, which the designer referred
to as a "park pavilion" because of
its closeness to nature and the
occasional hummingbird visitor.

ROOFTOPS

What greater freedom is there, than opening up one's home to the sky? City houses with roof access are highly coveted, and the rooftops are frequently adorned to create sparkling oases. More natural landscape can be seen from rooftops that are made comfortable for stargazing and communing with the big sky.

◄ Supported by Doric columns, a vine-covered pergola helps divide a tight, Manhattan penthouse terrace into sitting and dining areas. Brick-colored pavers slyly correspond to the brick buildings surrounding it, while the gray pergola echoes the beautifully weathered redwood furniture.

▲ Bright upholstery and many plants
in terra-cotta pots add color and
verve to a secluded roof deck.
The designer adds seating space
by transforming one side of
the perimeter railing into a
long banquette.

Paned doors lead to the simple roof deck. Weathered wood and rough plaster play counterpoint to the New Orleans French Quarter moldings and balustrade. A spiral staircase leads to the very top, where a hot tub and views of the community await.

A sunbathing roof is equipped with over-stuffed cushions on custom metal chaise lounges. The balustrade is topped with mirrored balls that reflect sunlight and scenery.

BREAKING FREE

What makes a room a room? Many people would say that a room contains at least one wall. But we are interested in spaces that defy such definitions. Just as it's not the structure that makes a house a home, it's not walls that make a space a room. Intimacy and intent are paramount criteria. Intimacy may be achieved in the grand outdoors by the furniture type and placement. Plants, ground cover, arbors, and trellises all contribute to create spaces that suggest comfort and feelings of freedom in the outdoors.

In Charles Baudelaire's imaginary garden, "There is nothing else but grace and measure,/Richness, quietness, and pleasure." For many homeowners, a beautiful garden space need not be imagined. By working with designers, architects, and landscapers who understand the terrain, you can enjoy quietness and pleasure in your own home.

A vast courtyard separates the glass-fronted main house from the guest house, and is flanked on either side by manifestations of water. The quiet lap pool on one side contrasts with the intriguing stairway on the other. Inset ponds with river rocks are a metaphor for a tranquil stream flowing to the sea.

COURTYARDS

Though bound by the walls of the house, well-designed courtyards evoke dual feelings of containment and expansion. While formal courtyards may be used for high-end entertaining, many West Coast homeowners use their courtyards as year-round dining—and even conference—spaces.

◀ Log beams on one side and trees on the other bolster this small, yet effective, space. Stone flooring creates a surface peninsula that supports the wrought-iron breakfast seating set. Rather than extend the stone to the stucco wall, the design includes a grassy area, which effectively makes the garden passage seem larger and also defines a separate area for casual dining.

◀ ▼ A two-part courtyard acts as a unifying space for this dual-structure home, with the gatehouse toward the front of the property, and the principal residence in the back with a southern exposure. Alternating plaster colors and different paving set the spaces apart, while the green trim throughout holds the look together.

◄ ◄ A colorful courtyard serves as dining and meeting space for the home and studio of graphic designer Charlie Hess, who, working closely with landscape designer Mayita Dinos, transforms a dirt pit into redwood-and-mosaic oasis. A brave mix of colors and materials, such as Mexican tile, pebbles, terra-cotta pavers, redwood, and painted and weathered teak, bring energy to a relatively small space.

▲ Rustic austerity describes this
remodel of a 1950s A-frame by the
owners/designers. Timber furniture
and rough-hewn stone contribute
to the rural French farmhouse style.
The courtyard has sweeping views
of the ocean, yet is made cozy by
the outdoor fireplace.

▲ The designer brings Spanish
Colonial Revival to her own home in
an expansive courtyard, complete
with fireplace, banquettes, and
several sitting and dining areas.
Early California artifacts, and her
own furniture designs, bring warmth
and intimacy to the large space.

▶ Several spaces on the brick-paved
courtyard are defined by their
furniture: a wicker deep-seating
group fosters long conversations;
antique wicker uprights form a
cozy tête-à-tête; a metal table
and chairs accommodate casual
dining; lounge chairs are protected
within the mock-Tudor porch;
and simple benches call for
solitary contemplation.

▶ The designer and photographer use the courtyard as a year-round dining room in their Hollywood Hills home, former manse of the famed costume designer Adrian. Strategic plantings, fireplace, and nearby fountain add charm and elegance.

◀ Creativity knows no bounds for the husband-and-wife design team who create a lush, cottage-like outdoor room in a 1930s Los Angeles housing complex. Where once was fake grass, now are terra-cotta pavers and a multitude of potted flowers and greenery. French bistro chairs add a delicate touch.

A banal lawn is transformed into an enchanted water room with lush koi pond and dining area. The bright colors echo the citrus trees as well as the Bauer pottery used as the fountain font. Mosaic table is by artist Nancy Kintisch.

▲ Elegant, Italian Renaissance—
inspired furniture groups border
a formal area designed for
entertaining. Contemplative
sculpture is a focal point, and
stone garden ornaments enhance
the stately, yet inviting, space.

▶ Bedroom, living room, and dining room form the walls of an outdoor living/dining room in the renovated home for landscape architect Rob Pressman. Concrete pavers are grouted with grass; broad steps leading down to the space double as amphitheater-like seating. The fireplace brings added warmth to the space.

◀ Carved out of a three-bedroom, hillside house, a simple courtyard provides hard- and soft-scape areas for the family. Living spaces open on the courtyard, which, like the rest of the house, is conceived from simple, yet elegant, materials.

A courtyard is visible through large windows in the entrance foyer, which separates two wings of the house. Rich ochre tones and wooden details are used to evoke the casual, yet vibrant, lifestyles of Napa Valley and Tuscany. The small, Romeo-and-Juliet balcony adds charm and whimsy.

Trellises

Arbors and trellises add a certain romance and Classicism to an outdoor space. The often-simple wood structures rein in an area and bring formality to processions and patios.

▲ ▶ A long arbor extends over the brick path from the pool, leading to the spa grotto. The spa is open to the sky, while side areas, paved with colored concrete, are screened by grape and wisteria on the arbor. Delicately intertwined metal furniture echoes the natural growth patterns of the overhead vines.

▲ Colored stucco columns support the trellis that casts dramatic shadows onto a bar-equipped entertainment space. Irregularly sized Idaho stone defines the space within the rest of the lawn-covered yard.

◄ ◄ Wooden trusses supported by terra-cotta columns define several areas of an expansive outdoor suite, which is fully transformed from a bland ranch-house exterior. Multilevel terraces paved in terra cotta and colored concrete accommodate entertaining and family dining. Built-in barbecue and fireplace further contribute to the use and flexibility of the space.

outdoor easy —
building an arbor trellis

In the classic movies, arbors are often the romantic rendezvous spots, where the leading lady and her man meet after dark for their first kiss—or maybe their last. In real life, arbors can range in size from small entrance ways covered with roses to large trellises protecting an entire table from patio or terrace in the heat of a summer day. A basic arbor is simple to construct.

Pressure-treated pine or naturally decay-resistant cedar are the most common materials used to construct an arbor. The goal is for the arbor to support the weight of the plants that will grow or be set upon it.

the design:

Decide upon the size and spacing of the rafters, as this determines the size of the support members. Rafters can be plain or fancy—ending in curves, notches, or elaborate scrollwork. The rafters can be left uncovered or covered with cloth, plants, lath, or lattice. In the design, you'll gain a sense of unity by repeating an architectural detail of the house, such as the pitch of a gable, window trim, railing pattern, or paint color. Arbors vary in height, but usually range from 8 feet to 10 feet. If covering the arbor with plants, leave plenty of headroom for the vines growing overhead to droop down. Also, when deciding upon the arbor's length and width, remember that a roof overhead always makes the floor space below seem smaller.

the construction:

Concrete footings will support the weight of the posts, arbor, and plants. Piers of cast concrete are embedded in poured concrete footings. Posts are 4-by-4 lumber or larger. Post-to-beam connections may need bracing. Metal anchors secure posts to piers or to a concrete slab. Rafters sit atop beams and are spaced for plant support or shade. Orientation determines the extent of shade cast below.

right
A wooden swing hanging in a small arbor creates an intimate retreat. Its architecture echos that of the main house. Vines cover the support columns.

GARDEN ROOMS

The most amorphous of room spaces are those that are set in gardens, with only natural elements and furnishings to define the space. Not merely gardens with benches, these outdoor rooms truly embrace warmth, intimacy, and design.

▶ ▶ Steel-and-teak furniture creates a serpentine counterpart to the square pavers for an energetic garden that lies between two, three-story buildings connected by a catwalk. A rock-garden border surrounds concrete pavers, with moss growing between the lines. The space is bordered by walls of steel, doors of white-painted pegboard and white acrylic sheeting, and sliding panels of medium-density fiberboard and acrylic sheeting.

▲ Potted and planted succulents
abound amid cactus-colored metal
chairs and tile-top table. The simple
placement of plants and furniture
creates a space for reflection.

Using flagstone as an area rug, famed Hollywood producer Robert Evans entertains guests such as Henry Kissinger and Dustin Hoffman under the hundreds-year-old sycamore tree, which, according to the owner "is more valuable than any painting I own." The stone slab has been the site of many parties, dances, and weddings, as well as intimate dinners around the wrought-iron table purchased in France.

The designer creates a lush garden fantasy for his own home with climbing roses and moss hiding a wooden gazebo. Refined iron furniture contrasts with a rustic twig chair.

Situated within a "ruined landscape," as the designer describes it, are several small seating areas. A fragmented wall appears to be the remains of a former structure, yet is newly designed and placed. This artistic display of water, stone, and flowers gives way to a more ordered patio.

◄ ▲ This 40-foot by 80-foot (12.2 meter by 24.4-meter) area is coined "the empty room" by the architect and homeowner for its simple definition of space bound on one side by a low, dry-mortar stone wall and on the other by a Richard Serra steel sculpture. The clean emptiness—ideal for contemplative afternoons—is even maintained with the addition of badminton space that is planted with a different type of sod to delineate the court area.

POOL SURROUNDS

The pool is a perfect example of captured nature—a pond of one's own, if you will. There is much more variety of shape and color in today's pools, and equal, if not greater, attention is paid to the areas surrounding them.

▲ The feelings of enclosure and protection are afforded by the spa pavilion of yellow and blue plaster. The open pool area is buttressed by the concrete bench along the water, and the garden wall, which stops the space from flowing into the landscape.

◄ ▲ Distinctions between sky, sea, and land disappear. A sky-blue pool is redesigned to overflow the cliff's edge and seemingly blend with the Pacific Ocean. The patio, surfaced with blue-green-gray concrete, is bound by low concrete seating walls and planted with succulents chosen for their dramatic profiles as well as their low maintenance.

◄ ▲ Narrow space necessitates creativity in the design and installation of this Tuscan-inspired pool and patio area in the Hollywood Hills. High walls on either side maintain a soft yellow color that corresponds with the stone paving, creating a delicate and open feeling. Stone planters, an Italianate fountain, and an ornamental obelisk give the feeling of a grand European garden, as does the tamed, trellised ivy and neatly manicured shrubs.

Melding into the earth tones of the Arizona desert, this strong, massive house presents its pool and outdoor room area as a place of further calm and contemplation. Bright desert hues of fuchsia and aqua are used sparingly, but to great effect, in the spa- and pool-tile detailing. A series of horizontal planes creates the illusion of a stacked horizon of water, wall, and mountain. A structure affording daytime shade, evening light, and heat relief rises above the informal dining area.

▼ Rustic, yet refined, twig and woven furniture defines several separate dining and seating areas. Twin pool-side dining pavilions are draped with muslin and support candle-filled iron chandeliers.

The designer's weekend home is an example of refined style. The square pool sits within its platform in a neat, geometric layout, almost like an Josef Albers painting. This quiet homage to the square gets energy from the many-hued fieldstone surrounding the pool. A continuity of materials is gained by using the same stone around the house. A casual, trellised breakfast area is just beyond the kitchen window.

▲ A stark stucco wall with large punched-out openings forms a dramatic backdrop for a hillside spa and seating area. Circular spa and irregularly shaped stones play in counterpoint to the strict angular geometry of the house and furniture.

◄ One of several entertainment terraces, the pool level sports a rich, monochromatic scheme in the flagstone, iron furniture, and deep taupe upholstery. Distinct areas form dining room, living room, and sitting area on this terrace that is equipped with sophisticated sound equipment.

◄ ▶ The designer furnishes the
outdoor space of her own home
with creative use of raw materials:
poured concrete legs support a
black-granite table top; smooth
concrete flooring is interrupted
by pool and pebbles; stained
concrete benches provide seating
and separation of vegetation area;
charcoal-stained concrete-block
bar supports a slate top; and
natural concrete-block wall
frames the yard. With the owner's
two dogs enjoying the yard,
planting grass was not an option,
so the designer opts for gravel
and pebbles.

▲ A bold, white-stucco wall, which acts as a backdrop to the outdoor dining room, creates a picture frame for the mountains. Taking the idea of a pool house to another dimension, the designer cantilevers a metal-mesh awning from the wall creating shade and protection from sun and wind. Redwood deck, concrete water fountain, grass inserts, and free-form rocks add to the geometric play.

◄ ◄ A stucco-and-timber trellis defines the terrace of a Mexican-inspired Los Angeles home. The outdoor pool area is the first vista seen by visitors as they walk through the glass-enclosed entry cube. The design of the house is shaped by dramatic rock formations and layered mountain ranges. Intense earth colors mirror the landscape and the sunsets around this house that sits so naturally in its site.

INSIDE OUT

A room outdoors can consist of four walls with an optional roof. It may have a roof with barely a hint of wall holding it up. Sometimes these rooms are stark, almost sculptural, and other times playful, harking back to the tradition of architectural follies. Others are decked out in full regalia, plush as the great indoors. All, however, are true outdoor rooms—single spaces that can be defined architecturally in the outdoors.

These spaces fulfill several functions. They may be strictly ornamental—a pretty pavilion in the garden. Often they are designed to complement the pool, servicing swimmers while providing shelter away from the house. Free from the constraints of the main house, single-room structures allow designers and architects greater freedom to experiment and express themselves in design, materials, and construction.

The designer creates a serene green retreat for her own Hollywood Hills home. A thatched trellis roof covers an outdoor dining room with a painted green interior and green-and-white furniture. A large mirror gives the illusion of more space by reflecting the dining room and the outdoor spaces beyond. The covered intimacy of the space allows the designer to use fine china and silver outdoors.

RETREATS

A private retreat, apart from the main house, allows
psychological as well as physical separation from the every day.
Used for reading, meditation, or work, these spaces are special
to their owners for their ability to restore and refresh.

This exquisite and daring outdoor folly reinterprets a Mexican walled garden in a series of boxes, gardens within gardens, and mysterious passageways, creating, in the words of the designer, "a metaphor of a house." Saturated colors and selected cacti heighten the desert atmosphere in this art/contemplation area, which is situated within an existing lush English-style garden in Texas. This project stretches the definitions of space, room, and garden. Rooms are filled only with space, while gardens are art galleries.

▼ ▶ Translucence and opacity are playfully combined in a greenhouse/garage on the architects' own property. Plastic sheets cover a wood-frame structure on the roof and two sides. The other two sides are made of wood, with windows in translucent plastic. The plastic walls are humorously equipped with opaque windows.

◀ Playfully called "Jabba the Hut" by the owner/architect, this 8-foot (2.5-meter) square room was designed with laminated glass, Douglas fir, redwood shingles, and copper siding. Front and back doors are made of four movable panels to provide variable ventilation options and allow the room to be as transparent as possible.

Pavilions and Gazebos

Flirting with mass, the trellis and fretwork of a delicate garden pavilion rejoices in openness. Ready-made gazebos are easily personalized with favorite furniture, while a custom design can often stand alone as a stark and mysterious structure.

▶ Designed as a vista view from the main house balcony, this intimate garden space is outfitted with a steeply pitched shingle-roof gazebo, highlighted by a finial from the owner, a garden antiques dealer. White iron furniture contributes to the light, graceful feeling inside the gazebo, while a rustic, twig-inspired iron bench rests on the herringbone brick patio.

A string of potted citrus trees leads to two intersecting semicircular volumes—one of Bouquet Canyon stone, the other of white steel framework—that provide a seating and contemplation area in this artistically designed vegetable garden. The stone retaining wall serves as a waterfall, allowing a continual flow of water to seep through the cracks. The vegetable plot is sectioned into discreet units, stratified into different levels.

◀ ▲ Built as a retreat for the architect and friends just outside Joshua Tree National Monument in the California desert, this remarkable structure includes a geometric gazebo painted in the burnt orange of desert blooms. Openings of irregular shapes in the stucco walls frame views of the high desert.

◄ ▲ A steel-frame hexagon trellis wrapped with a forty-year-old vine forms the ceiling for an entertainment gazebo with a city view. The concrete floor is finished for a terrazzo look, and the fireplace is clad with rough, high-desert stone. The bar counter is clad with copper and topped with stainless steel.

▲ A formal garden gazebo is the focal point for breakfast, afternoon tea, or entertaining. The owners replace a wooden floor with a sunburst brick pattern, and furnish the space with all-weather wicker seating.

▶ Santa Rita stone and grass replace concrete decking around the pool, which is situated at the lower level of a sloping lot. The pergola provides a shaded reading and resting area by the pool and a visual resting point from the upper-level terraces and the country club beyond.

◄ ▲ A garden pavilion's raised-deck flooring—complete with painted rug—and dropped-canvas ceiling add greater illusion to the interior hand-painted canvas panels. Carved redwood furniture repeats flora and fauna motifs found in the fabrics, accessories, and wall paintings. Full-height curtained openings leading to a stone balustrade, and the canvas-backed lattice work, contribute to the play of indoor and outdoor.

outdoor easy — installing the gazebo or summerhouse

Like potting sheds, gazebos can be do-it-yourself projects. Relatively simple structures, gazebos require a foundation, posts or walls, beams, rafters, and roofing. Height should be at least 8 feet at the highest point and the foundation should be at least 8 feet wide and deep to provide sufficient space for furniture. A traditional 6- or 8-hub style shape is easiest to construct. Pressure-treated lumber will resist decay. Solid roof materials should be pitched to allow water runoff.

Gazebos can, in fact, be quite fancy. Add gingerbread trim from the Victorian era. Try an octagonal or hexagonal shape, rather than a square or round structure. Or have some fun. Hire an artist or an architect—or design your own unique gazebo or small shelter that stands as a piece of sculpture in your garden. Try using unusual materials, such as plywood or stone or twigs. Designate the gazebo as the location for the cigar smokers in the house. Or build the treehouse that you always wanted as a kid. If you are weak of heart, gazebo kits are available.

A summerhouse is a more complicated to construct because you need to prepare a solid and level foundation of compacted hardcore material, approximately 4 inches (10 cm) thick. Over this foundation a concrete base is laid. (Or for a lightweight building, lay wooden bearers.) A summerhouse should be large enough to accommodate several people sitting comfortably, with doors opening out onto a veranda. You can design and make your own summerhouse, or summerhouses are available as prefabricated sectional buildings.

right
Dinner is served under a minimally designed gazebo, which consists of a roof and its supports—and a ceiling fan to move the air and spotlights pointed up into the ceiling for indirect lighting. The gazebo's simplicity is offset by the exotic setting.

POOL HOUSES

Our national monuments are reflected by water, so why not our own homes? Pool houses offer estate-like vistas as well as warm shelter after a relaxing dip.

▶ ▶ ▶ Set deep into the slope of the hillside, this sandstone-faced pool house includes a bath, sauna, and roof-top terrace. The rough-hewn, yet tightly constructed, stone pool-surround, platform, and steps leading to the pool house correspond with the lighter texture sandstone and teak pocket doors. Within the main pool house space, the stone flooring continues in the stark, meditative room whose concrete ceiling is dotted with glass cylinders through which a pattern of light passes. Emphasizing its placement in the hill slope, the pool house's side steps lead to the roof deck.

◄ ▲ The pool house for the noted fashion designer Adrienne Vittadini is a rich dramatic setting made comfortable with lush drapes and upholstered furniture. The architect combines English garden tradition with Italian country design, including hints of Palladian and Shingle-style architecture.

◀ ▼ Belying its East Coast location, this traditional and stately pool house has whimsical and unexpected touches in its fountain frond finials and mischievous squirrel ornament. Exterior curtains and welcoming decorative lintel lead the visitor into the exquisite and mannered interior. Mixing wrought-iron furniture from the 1940s with a nineteenth-century French campaign bed and Empire mirror, the designer combines comfort, whimsy, and elegance.

▲ Lattice work and formal garden
structure contribute to this
poolside pavilion. Wicker furniture,
lush fabrics, and plenty of
accessories bring warmth and
comfort to the backyard hideaway.

Set in a private arboretum, this indoor pool is connected to a Victorian residential complex by extended concrete walls. A serpentine stone wall contrasts with the angularly articulated glass and aluminum walls for an indoor pool. The irregularly shaped pool evokes a tamed river and continues outside to the fern-filled glen. Constant plays of contradictions—inside/outside, mechanical/natural, solid/liquid—abound in this remarkable structure.

DECORATIVE ELEMENTS

What and how many decorative accents to include in an outdoor room is a highly personal preference. Sculpture and other artworks can add an element of surprise. You can choose pieces that link indoors to outdoors. Or you can choose decorative accents that are decidedly made for outdoors—birdbaths, birdhouses, and wind chimes. Found objects can bring an eclectic flavor, while all types of pots and containers add a colorful touch.

Outdoor spaces can be showrooms displaying your favorite art. And that art can be abstract or classical sculpture, found objects, or even pieces of furniture. Visit the great public sculptural garden museums for inspiration. Either the entire space can be a gallery, or the artwork can be a focal point. Lighting becomes an essential ingredient, as the art should be quite visible at night. The artistic object could be the surprise element in your outdoor room.

Consider what artwork, if any, you would like to hang it in your screened in porch or in your sunroom. And, while you are at it, think of all the decorative value of all materials around you—the ceilings, flooring, and walls. How those surfaces are finished will affect the long-term enjoyment of the outdoor room.

Exotic plants, either planted in the ground or in planters, can provide drama. After all, the more exotic are usually more difficult to grow, so you might as well show off your horticultural skills. At night, the shapes of the plants will be more distinctive spotlighted against a blank, hard wall surface.

When choosing objects, scale is perhaps most important, particularly if the decorative element is going to be a focal point, such as a piece of sculpture. Consider mass as well as size. Simplicity and harmony with the other design elements are key considerations. The repetition of some elements will add to a sense of unity. Adequate lighting is a necessity and can play an important role in mood setting.

left and right
Choose from an array of decorative options. Strive for simplicity and harmony among design elements.

arranging pots

Make a dramatic statement with a grouping of container pots—planted or not. Rather than setting pots here and there on your terrace or deck, try congregating several of the same type (but not necessarily the same size) in one corner. Massed together, and perhaps lit at night, the effect can be quite pleasing. Usually the larger the pots, the better. This will also aid you, in that the plants will not dry out so quickly, and will need less attention. Of course, one large pot, planted with a variety of flowers can be lovely. Choose from containers of terra-cotta, stoneware, stone, wood, plastic, fiberglass, or metal, realizing that each will react somewhat differently to environmental conditions.

FILLING UP

A revolution has occurred in modern furniture with the emphasis on more casual living. These days, outdoor spaces are furnished with as much attention as those indoors. Manufacturers are designing and producing materials in sophisticated styles resulting in investment-quality furniture. Indoor/outdoor qualities are important, too, as homeowners desire flexibility and value.

▶ Architectural columns add to the Neo-Classical flavor of the Empress arm chair, designed by John Caldwell for The Veneman Collection, and evoke early nineteenth-century Empire-style furniture.

◀ Knoll presents PaperClip café tables created by Vignelli Designs as a companion to the classic Bertoia side chair, both exhibiting lightness of form and graphic lines.

HISTORICAL

From Classical to Neo-Classical, historical styles are ever popular in outdoor furniture and accessories. Victorian and Nantucket motifs are traditional for outdoors, but designers are turning to ancient, Renaissance, and nineteenth-century styles as well.

▼ Pairing two legendary Italian eras, Capital Garden Products presents the Medici Vase on the Pompeii Pedestal, which resemble ancient stone but are fabricated from fiberglass.

▲ Hand-carved chair and side table of redwood with a silvery weathered finish from Reed Bros. Europa Collection add European elegance to the garden.

▼ Harking back to early nineteenth-century campaign furniture, John Kelly designs a folding umbrella chair that allows for rest and shade anywhere one travels.

▶ Haddonstone's Corinthian column well head is manufactured in the tradition of English garden ornaments but uses specially treated and cast reconstructed limestone.

◄ Venus (from Sandro Botticelli's masterpiece) is interpreted in tile mosaic by artist Annie Sabroux, who creates custom, site-specific works.

▲ A nineteenth-century French olive jar is reproduced by The Elegant Earth and given a mottled patina to simulate age and use.

 ► Fifty pieces comprise the Renaissance collection designed by Enrique Gamboa in cast aluminum with antique finishes by Terra Furniture.

◄ Neo-Classical styling with Spanish overtones informs the design of the Isabella collection in cast aluminum by John Caldwell for Tropitone.

▲ Exuding Edwardian charm, this
bench, a replica of one designed by
Sir Edwin Lutyens in the early 1900s
for the gardens at Sissinghurst
Castle, is offered today by Barlow
Tyrie in plantation-grown teak.

▲ Intricate Aegean mosaic area rugs
from Ann Sacks Tile & Stone are
designed by Ellen Williamson and
made from naturally colored and
shaped stones.

▲ French artist Jacques Lamy harks
back to Neo-Classical shapes for his
collection of benches, urns, and
pedestals from Archiped Classics in
cast stone, with bronze components.

▲ Cathedral arches are shaped in
wrought aluminum for the Gothic
two-seater bench from McKinnon
and Harris.

ROMANTIC

Flowers and baskets, swooping graceful lines, and traditional styles bring romance and lazy summer days to mind. Outdoors is where wonder and imagination are expressed best through wicker and wood.

▼ Delicate candle sconces are offered by The Elegant Earth, which reproduces the design from a nineteenth-century French original.

▲ Abstracted flowers, drooping petals, and gilt accents define Flora dinnerware by Ann Morhauser of Annieglass in slumped glass painted white for a porcelain-like effect.

▶ A classic ocean liner steamer with solid brass fittings, made by Kingsley-Bate, adjusts to four positions and folds for compact storage.

This Ram's Head urn by Capital Garden Products is made of lightweight fiberglass that is imbedded with bronze powder to effect a natural patina finish.

Painterly illusion abounds in Annie Sabroux's custom tile mural that brings beauty and depth to an outdoor niche.

This charming flower basket with haut relief along the rim is made of Haddonstone's reconstituted limestone, which is tested and treated for outdoor endurance.

▼ Weatherend's Quarter Circle settee is inspired by furniture found at a turn-of-the-century Maine coast estate and is updated using marine-grade paint on mahogany.

▲ The Front Porch collection from Lloyd/Flanders presents all the traditional charm of wicker furniture in its noted all-weather wicker made from paper-wrapped woven wires dipped in weatherproof coating.

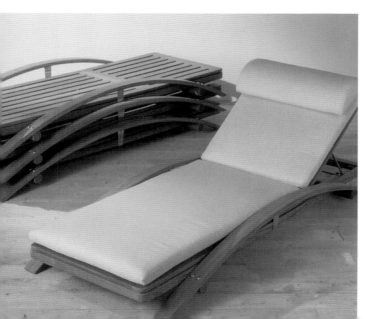

▲ Sonoma, designed John Caldwell for Tropitone, presents grapevine and leaf motifs in cast aluminum.

◀ The Sun Deck adjustable stacking chaise from Summit Furniture is infused with grace and style by yacht stylist John Munford.

▼ Delicately styled Gabrielle café chairs and tables are made from flat iron-bar stock with a powder-coat finish in Europe for Wickets Garden Style.

▲ The Essex tea trolley from Windsor Designs is made from Shorea wood, a mahogany-like hardwood that is stronger, heavier, and more plentiful than teak.

▶ The Eastlake collection by Brown Jordan evokes lazy days associated with wicker furniture but has a modern twist—the wicker is constructed from resin imbedded with ultraviolet inhibitors.

◄ Traditional construction techniques and modern technology come together in the Glenham circular tree seat from Barlow Tyrie, made of plantation-grown, all-weather teak that is cut to shape, rather than bent or steamed.

▲ Mottahedeh offers Tulip earthenware plates, cups, and saucers reproduced from originals in the Museum of Decorative Arts, Paris.

◄ Graceful curves abound in Lawrence Peabody's Gatsby design for Terra Furniture made of cast aluminum.

RUSTIC

Timber and twig furniture truly form a connection with nature. Rustic looks also include materials such as stone and reclaimed barnwood. Some manufacturers even offer the illusion of rustication in clever designs and materials.

▲ Naturally weathered wood is used to make Frontier Barnwood's Strong Box planter.

▲ The classic Adirondack chair—this one from Richardson Allen—continues to be an all-time favorite for its deep seating comfort and relaxed look.

◄ The simple, honest form of these Long Toms is derived from nineteenth-century tomato pots and is made today in English terra cotta by Kinsman Company.

▲ Through state-of-the-art graphic technology, Imagine Tile produces ceramic floor tiles that present photo images of the outdoors.

▲ The Harvest table is from Barnwood Originals, which disassembles abandoned barns and reuses the historical wood.

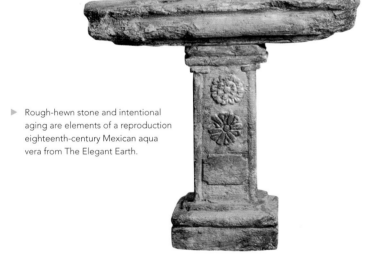

▶ Rough-hewn stone and intentional aging are elements of a reproduction eighteenth-century Mexican aqua vera from The Elegant Earth.

▶ The raw properties of concrete are put to good use in table tops made from an ecologically designed, lightweight concrete material known as Syndecrete.

▶ Ancient designs from Crete inspire the oil jar and beehive jar, while an 1850 piece is the model for the battle urn, all of which are made of lightweight fiberglass by Capital Garden Products.

▲ Il Piata paving stones from Ann Sacks Tile & Stone feature mottled design and color in frostproof material.

▶ Carmel seating recalls the smooth touch of weathered driftwood but is made of sand-cast aluminum in a design by John Caldwell for The Veneman Collection.

◀ Old Hickory's log-inspired Grove Park chair and ottoman combine with the Cricket table for a rich cabin look.

▲ Kim Hansen creates custom tile-and-stone tables for Casual Comforts in a variety of shapes, sizes, and colors.

◀ Resembling rough-hewn stone, the Alpine trough is made of cast, reconstituted limestone, and may be used on matching supports by Haddonstone or placed directly on the ground.

MEDITERRANEAN/ISLAND

Hot weather and clear, blue water evoke days of island pleasure. Rich colors and textures recall Mediterranean vacations (or dreams).

▲ Created in Australia, the Down Under hanging pot from Kinsman Company is hand-crafted of natural terra cotta in the United States.

▲ Giati's Alisèo teak chair was designed by Mark Singer for a five-star Hawaiian hotel expressly for use on the lanais and features adjustable elements that make it appropriate for dining as well.

▲ Dez Ryan's Island Denizen hurricane lamp is handmade by the artist/designer and includes a blown glass globe and bright glass beads dangling from a leafy collar.

▶ Xavier Llongueras makes this large, sunburst-patterned coffee table from hand-cut pieces of Byzantine glass inlay resting on a base of brushed steel for Catalonia Collections.

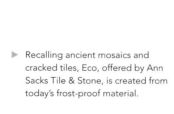

◀ Waves undulate in the back of Provence dining chairs in cast aluminum, designed by John Caldwell for Tropitone.

▶ Recalling ancient mosaics and cracked tiles, Eco, offered by Ann Sacks Tile & Stone, is created from today's frost-proof material.

◀ Torquay porcelain serving pieces from Mottahedeh are decorated with images of sea life.

▶ Hand-crafted by Ann Morhauser for Annieglass, the Shell series evokes natural sea forms and is made from sandblasted glass reminiscent of found beach glass; gold edges add formality.

◄ Recalling rattan furnishings, Jardin tables, cushion chairs, and chaise lounges by Brown Jordan are made from resin weaving material over aluminum frames.

▼ Terra-cotta pavers are brought up to date by Fiberstars, which uses fiber optic technology to incorporate lighting in its FiberScape paver system.

▲ Bamboo style is reinterpreted in cast aluminum stalks and leaves in a line of seating and tables designed by John Caldwell for The Veneman Collection.

WHIMSY

Outdoor living can't be taken too seriously, and these clever, lighthearted chairs, accessories, and tiles make adding joy and fun to your day easier.

▶ Majestic's Tulip Torches designed by David Tisdale stand pretty in their pots on tables and may also be accompanied by tulip string lights overhead.

▲ Topiary Series tiles from Ann Sacks Tile & Stone complement any garden setting with its green hues and charming illustrations of trees, birds, gardeners, and tools.

◀ Ironic in the extreme, Imagine Tile's Water design creates a pool-like illusion in glazed ceramic tile using up-to-date graphic technology.

▶ Richard Schultz evokes carved-and-shaped shrubbery in his Topiary designs in bent, stamped, and folded sheet aluminum available in clear or green finishes.

▼ Ann Morhauser of Annieglass designs Splash expressly for outdoor entertaining in fun fish shapes for bowls, platters, and plates.

▲ Inherently playful, this chess table is made from hand-cut marble by Xavier Llongueras for Catalonia Collections.

▲ Fluid shapes in polished aluminum give an almost animated feeling to the Toledo Collection of tables and chairs designed by Jorge Pensi for Knoll.

▲ Include an outdoor froggy friend on your table with this porcelain pitcher from Mottahedeh.

◄ Tiles are imbedded with recycled elements—such as twigs, nails, and glass chips—and made from Syndecrete, a lightweight concrete material developed by David Hertz, AIA.

GEOMETRIC

Contemporary geometric furniture embraces many forms and materials, from cast aluminum to traditional teak. Sleek, clean lines blend well with outdoor spaces that are kept simple and spare.

▶ Mesa from Brown Jordan exhibits sophisticated styling in teak chairs and tables that are available in rectangular and circular shapes; tables come with a slate inset.

▼ These pre-cast planters embody pure forms. David Hertz, AIA, designed them and made them from Syndecrete, the lightweight concrete material he developed.

▲ Aptare's first outdoor line, the Laguna Collection designed by Lawrence O'Toole, includes deep-seating sofa, arm chair, and low table made of plantation-grown solid teak.

▶ Crisp, contemporary design and white finish of the Perception line by Tropitone complement Modern homes.

▲ Orlando Diaz-Azcuy uses a trellis motif—intersecting solid teak members framed by circular and rectangular backs—in the Portico Collection of indoor/outdoor furniture for McGuire.

▲ Plastic Tabletop drinkware for the outdoors is designed in simple shapes by David Tisdale and manufactured by Majestic.

▲ Concentric circles shape the Adams top for the wrought-aluminum Hepplewhite side and coffee tables by McKinnon and Harris.

◄ Ilan Dei's cast aluminum Airfoil vase takes its dynamic shape from ship masts and is available in brushed, polished, and colored aluminum finishes.

▼ Teak furniture with cane inserts defines Giati's Azia line of tables and seating, which has stylistic echoes of both Asian and European design.

▲ Cool elegance and bright colors are hallmarks of Annieglass, designed by Ann Morhauser, whose long boats and triangle plates are handmade from slumped glass.

▶ Straight lines are softened by subtle curves in the Nantucket chaise made of solid teak by Kingsley-Bate.

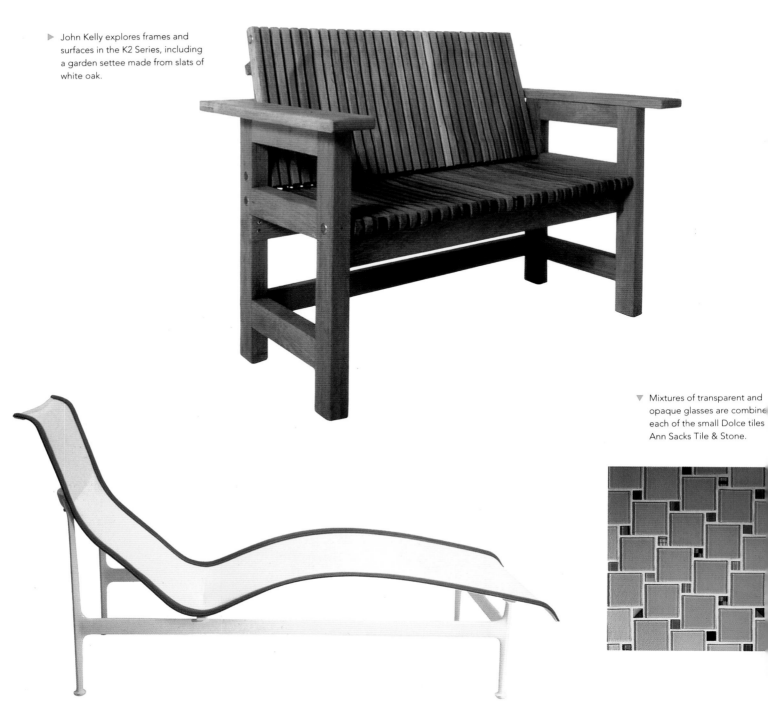

▷ John Kelly explores frames and surfaces in the K2 Series, including a garden settee made from slats of white oak.

▽ Mixtures of transparent and opaque glasses are combined each of the small Dolce tiles Ann Sacks Tile & Stone.

▲ A beautifully arced arabesque outlines the award-winning 1966 Collection by Richard Schultz in vinyl mesh on cast and extruded aluminum frames.

▷ Slatted apron detailing and curved benches are hallmarks of the mahogany Weatherend dining set, which uses full mortise-and-tenon joinery reinforced with marine-grade epoxy.

▲ The Drayton teak bench from Chelsea Ex-Centrics, constructed with traditional mortise-and-tenon joints and teak dowels, adds practicality with optional, detachable side tables.

Hand-crafted in England from solid, all-weather teak, the London design dates back to the early 1920s, when it was first offered by Barlow Tyrie.

▶ High verticality is featured in Summit Furniture's Sources dining chairs, which complement the First Cabin dining table, all designed by Kipp Stewart.

outdoor easy — easy fountains

The sound and sight of water can be a refreshing addition to an outdoor room. British designer and author Sir Terence Conran goes so far as to suggest that "a garden without water is a place that lacks soul." He argues that water adds drama, depth, excitement, mystery, and the lure of the natural world.

Fountains, waterfalls, and pools can be quite exotic. Moving water heightens the sense of a lush paradise as it gurgles and rushes and drowns out urban noise. Fountains can be beautifully crafted and become the focal point of an outdoor room. Choose from among bell and dome fountains, rotating or geyser nozzles, wall or bubble fountains. To gain full advantage, be sure the fountain is spotlit creatively at night. Ponds add a visual splash, for those who love gazing at water and aren't near the sea or a lake. For color, fill a pond with goldfish or water lilies, umbrella grass, or horsetail rush. Perhaps even more sensational than cooling off on a hot afternoon in the swimming pool is the atmosphere created by the reflection at nighttime of underwater lighting. Even the light emanating from a hot tub changes a typical deck into an exotic outdoor room.

While ponds, fountains, and waterfalls can be quite elaborate, it's also possible to start small—to get your toes wet before jumping into the deep end.

Try creating a basic fountain from a wooden planter, metal basin, or large ceramic pot. Line the container with a flexible material or coat the inside with asphalt emulsion or epoxy paint. Place a submersible pump with a riser pipe within the container and run the cord through the drain hole. Conceal and protect the cord by running it through a plastic conduit to a grounded electrical outlet. Use a cork to plug the drain hole and hold the cord in place. Seal both sides of the hole with silicone sealant. Dry overnight and then add water. Plug in the cord. Presto. You have a working fountain.

For the design of a formal pond, British horticulturalist John Brookes recommends the following: Use waterproof concrete. Include in the design an overflow pipe to prevent flooding and an outlet to a separate drainage field to allow for occasional cleaning. Where frost is light, use reinforced concrete and build the pool with sloping sides so that as the water freezes and turns into ice, it has room to expand. In colder areas you may need to empty to pool entirely to prevent frost damage. Pool copings should rise above the water by at least 2 inches (5 cm) to hide any change in the water level due to evaporation, and to conceal the green algae strains that inevitably occur where a surface meets the water.

OUTDOOR DECORATING PROJECTS: STEP-BY-STEP

the basics

HARVESTING

For all of the projects in this book, the first and perhaps most important step is selecting and harvesting the botanicals. Always choose blossoms and plants in peak condition, as the drying process will only intensify any flaws. If you are buying from a florist, ask to be shown the freshest flowers available. If you are harvesting from your own garden, choose flowers and leaves that are fully open. An exception is roses, which you may wish to harvest with partially opened buds.

It's also important to make sure the flowers are dry. No matter how beautiful they may look in the morning dew or with droplets of water glistening on their petals after an unexpected shower, do not pick flowers and other botanicals when they are wet. Extra moisture can cause discoloring, mold, and rapid deterioration in quality. On bright days, late morning is often the best time for harvesting. The afternoon hours are also fine as long as it doesn't get too hot and the blossoms appear healthy and not wilted.

It's smart not to harvest more than you can dry or press on that same day. Whichever preservation method you choose, begin as soon after harvesting as possible, certainly no more than an hour or two. Immediately after harvesting is ideal. Always harvest more pieces for drying than you will need for your project. Some will dry better than others, or you may be inspired to craft more and will appreciate having the extras.

It's also a good idea to keep a record of your flowers or botanicals, including where and when you picked them. Such information might prove helpful if you want to go back another year to find more. You might also want to incorporate plant information into the craft itself; for instance, you might paste a dried flower on a note card and add its botanical name in calligraphic lettering. If a dried item has a particular memory attached to it, such as a walk in the woods with a friend, you might want to keep track of it so that you can use it to make a personal gift for your friend.

Whether you grow your own botanicals or visit your favorite florist or farm stand to collect them, be sure to consult "The Inside Dirt"—a special tip box accompanying each project in this book—for insights and shortcuts on harvesting and handling. For more in-depth information on growing and drying specific flowers, consult one of the many books currently available on this subject.

DRYING

There are several ways to go about drying flowers, herbs, and other plant materials for craft use. The method you choose may depend on the resources you have at hand or it may be dictated by the craft project itself. Always read the instructions and get a feel for the scope of a project before purchasing or collecting materials. Three popular methods for drying flowers and other botanicals, including how they work and under what circumstances they work best, are outlined here.

Air-Drying

Air-drying is exceptionally easy. It requires little attention and few, if any, special resources. A bonus is the decorative accent air-dried botanicals lend to the home. Air-drying can be accomplished in several ways, depending on the material being dried. No matter which method you use, several important guidelines apply:

- Dry plant material in a relatively dark part of the house, as sunlight will fade the color.

- Avoid areas that are moist. That rules out basements, kitchens, and bathrooms. Suitable places can include attics, large closets, a garage, or a garden shed. If you live in a relatively humid climate or if you are drying during a wet or humid time of year, run a dehumidifier in the drying area.

- Choose a well-ventilated space. Air needs to be able to circulate around objects left to dry to preserve them effectively.

Hanging

Hanging flowers to dry takes nothing more than a twist-tie to clasp the flowers in bundles, plus string and a hook or nail from which to hang them. The drawback is that natural drying takes time, from one week up to a month or more, depending on the plant material. It is most effective with herbs and compact flowers, such as peony buds, rosebuds, safflower buds, delphiniums, chive flowers, and partially opened marigolds. It is not the optimum choice for flowers that readily shed their petals, such as black-eyed Susans or daisies. Flowers with delicate structures that could be compromised when bunched together should also not be dried in this fashion. Here are the basics:

- Assemble the flowers in small bundles, about eight to ten stems each. If the bundles are too bulky, the flowers or plant material in the interior may not properly dry.

- Bundle the same kind of flowers together. Choose flowers that are the same size and at the same stage of blossoming for each bundle, so that they dry at an even rate.

- Bind the bundled stems together at the cut end with a twist-tie. String also works, but a twist-tie is more readily tightened as the stems dehydrate and shrink.

- Tie string around each bundle and hang from a hook or nail.

- Examine the stems for an excess of leaves, and pull some or all of them off. Usually, there are more leaves on a stem than look attractive once dry. Also, a cluttering of leaves can impede the flow of air. If you're undecided on how much to trim off, use discretion. You can pull off more leaves after they are dry.

Screen

Screen-drying is ideal for flowers that splay out flat, such as cosmos, anemones, fever-few, and daisies, and for bulky flowers that might be compressed or disfigured if hung upside down. It is also the preferred way to dry individual petals.

The technique is simple: Prop an old window screen horizontally on a couple of sawhorses or crates. To dry whole flowers, insert the stem down through the mesh weave so that the flower rests on top of the screen. Don't place the flowers too closely together, and make sure none of the petals or leaves overlap. The air must be able to circulate freely on all sides for effective, even drying.

If the weave on a screen is too fine for running stems through, clip larger openings with wire cutters. You can also improvise with larger, more open wire meshes, such as chicken wire. If the blossom on a flower is too small or delicate to hang from a larger mesh, slip a large paper clip up the stem to straddle the mesh. For a small decorative screen, try holding cheesecloth taut in an embroidery hoop.

Naturally

Some flowers dry practically on their own. Everlastings, as the name implies, are particularly well suited to natural drying. All you need to do is set the flowers in a vase with about ½" (1 cm) of water to start. The water will be absorbed and evaporate in no time, and the flowers will continue to dry on their own. Other flowers well-suited to this no-nonsense approach include strawflowers, hydrangeas, globe amaranth, yarrow, heather, Chinese lanterns, baby's breath, statice, and honesty. Ornamental grasses also drape nicely when dried this way.

Using Desiccants

Another method for drying flowers is to cover them with a drying agent, or desiccant. The most popular desiccant in use today is silica gel, a sandlike substance available from garden stores, craft supply stores, and some florists under a variety of trade names. It is ideal for drying flowers because it works relatively quickly and effectively—the drying time can range from three to seven days—and it preserves the color and shape of the item being dried.

To use silica gel, you will need several airtight containers. Limit each container to one type of flower or plant material at a time, to avoid having different kinds of materials drying at different rates. Place ½" (1 cm) to 1" (3 cm) of silica gel in the bottom of the container to create a base. Trim off the stem, leaving 1" (3 cm) to 2" (5 cm), and then proceed as follows:

1 | Place flat-faced flowers, such as Gerber daisies, facedown into the silica gel.

2 | Lay bell-shaped or spiked flowers, such as snapdragons, horizontally on their sides.

3 | Place flowers with many layers of overlapping petals, such as dahlias, peonies, and marigolds, faceup on the gel. Carefully sprinkle granules in between the overlapping petals, using tweezers to gently lift and separate the layers, if necessary.

Make sure none of the flowers that are placed on the gel touch or overlap one another. Then gently sift more silica gel over and around the flowers until they are fully covered. Work slowly, so that the petals remain in their natural position and are not crushed. Add more layers of flowers and silica gel if space permits.

Close the container, and add a label with the date and flower name. Store the container in a relatively dark, dry area of the house, but in view, so that you will remember to check it periodically. Begin checking on the second day of drying. Delicate flowers with thin petals may dry in just under three days. Bulkier flowers could take as long as one week.

4 | When the flowers or plant materials are crisp and feel dry, carefully remove the silica gel, and pull out the dried items with tweezers. Any dusty residue can be removed with a soft, dry artist's brush. To reuse the silica gel, simply dehydrate it in the oven, following the manufacturer's instructions.

Many projects in this book require flowers in two-dimensional form—that is, they need to be pressed. Botanicals particularly well suited to pressing include ferns, leaves, and flowers with thin petals and little layering—pansies, clematis, violas, lobelia, delphiniums, and petunias, for example. Flowers with many layers of petals, such as zinnias and peonies, can be pressed by disassembling the flower into individual petals. Once the petals are pressed dry, they can be reassembled to mimic the form of the flower or used separately as accents.

Like the other drying methods, pressing is easy to do. If you're just learning to press flowers or plan to press only a small amount, you can easily do so with books. Set the items to be pressed between two sheets of blotting paper, or other absorbent paper, and place the sandwiched layers between the pages of a large, heavy book, such as a telephone directory. You will only be able to insert a few pages of pressed flowers in a book before it gets bulky and presses ineffectively. Weigh down the book with additional books or some other flat, heavy object, such as a cast-iron pan.

A flower press has decided advantages over the book method. If you do your harvesting on hikes in the woods, you can take a small press along with you and begin the pressing process immediately. Another advantage to using a press is that it is orderly. When you press flowers and botanicals between the pages of various books, it's easy to lose track of them.

Professional flower presses come with blotting paper and cardboard sheets. To use a press, place the flowers and plant matter between the sheets of blotting paper. Stack these "sandwiches," interleaved with the cardboard sheets, on the press bed. Put the top back on the press and tighten until the layers are held secure. Wait at least a week before checking the progress of your pressed items. If the plant or flower is not yet completely dry, put it back in the press for another five to seven days. Once the flower is dry, lift it with tweezers. If it sticks, use the tip of a paring knife or craft knife to gently lift it.

For better flower drying:

• Place flowers and other plant material facedown on the blotting paper.

• Choose items of equal thickness to press together.

• Do not allow plant materials to touch each other.

• If the base of a flower is bulky, use small scissors to trim off as much
  as possible on the stem side without causing any of the petals to fall off.

• If the flower is delicate but has a thick stem, avoid air pockets by either
  cutting off the stem to dry separately or slicing down the stem with a craft
  knife to create a flatter surface.

• Let the stems bow or curve as they are inclined. Straight lines can look
  stiff and unnatural.

STORING AND PRESERVING

All dried botanicals should be stored between layers of tissue paper in sealed containers or cardboard boxes. It cannot hurt to include a sprinkling of silica gel on the bottom of the box or container to absorb any lingering moisture or humidity. Pressed flowers may be stored between sheets of tissue paper in a large, manila envelope, along with a cardboard insert to prevent bending. Always label and date your packages, and store them away from sunlight, insects, and sources of moisture.

Use similar logic with any projects you craft from your dried flowers, leaves, or other plant material. Display finished projects in a relatively dry part of the house unless, of course, the dried item has been protected with a sealer coat, such as in decoupage.

To help preserve dried flowers, you can apply a light coat of hair spray or clear lacquer spray, available in craft stores. If a flower seems delicate and likely to fall apart, put a drop of clear-drying glue at the blossom center and on the back of flower base, where the petals connect to the stem.

Pressed flowers tend to fade, even when properly stored. They can be brightened with watercolors. Simply place the flower on a paper towel and lightly touch up with water-thinned paint, brushing from the center outward.

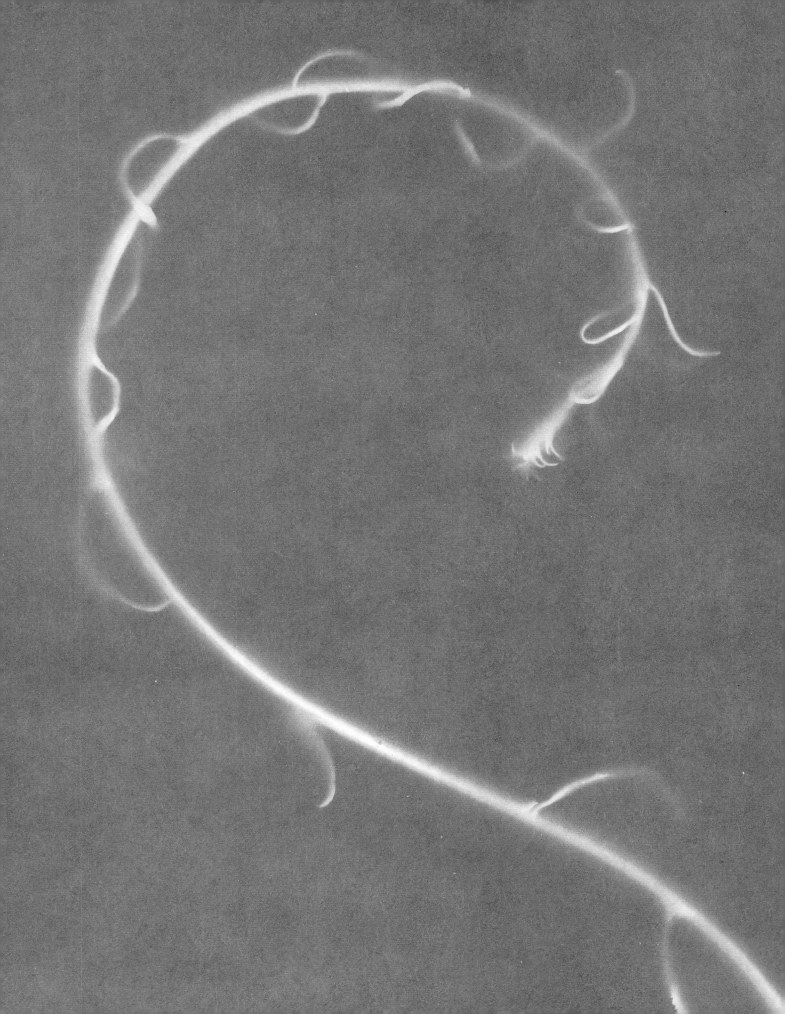

This chapter is all about capturing brilliant seasonal colors in bloom before they fade into a state of winter rest. Cluster romantically rich red roses (from the garden or from an admirer) into the suiting shape of a heart set in a shadow box. Dot everyday terra-cotta flowerpots with the cheerful faces of pansies, plentiful in both spring and fall. Or, wrap your favorite, most vibrant botanicals around handmade clay napkin rings to brighten the dinner table long after a fresh bouquet would have wilted.

colors in bloom

This is just a sampling of the everyday objects that can be enhanced with colors at peak bloom. Many of the projects in this chapter use flowers that air-dry particularly well. Sunlight will quickly fade color brilliance, so if you do air-dry your selections, be sure to choose a dark, dry location with ample air circulation. For more details on pressing and drying, refer to The Basics, beginning on page 187.

rose heart shadow boxes

Garden roses provide the vivid colors in these folk art–inspired shadow boxes. If you are cutting your own roses for this project, wait until the morning dew has dried. If you are purchasing roses from a florist, look for youthful, well-formed heads with no signs of mold.

MATERIALS

dried roses in two or three shades*

unfinished wood shadow boxes*

dry floral foam

dark mahogany wood stain

craft acrylic paint in cream and green

clear furniture paste wax

dark bronze dry artist's pigment

low-temperature glue gun

glue sticks

hair dryer

sharp knife

scissors

foam brushes

fine sandpaper

clean, soft cloths

*Approximately 36 red garden roses and 30 yellow spray roses fill the 6" x 6" (15 cm x 15 cm) shadow box at the far right

1 | Paint each shadow box, applying dark mahogany stain as a base coat followed by two coats of cream or green acrylic paint; let dry after each coat. Sand off some of the paint along the edges to reveal the underlying stain. To further age the boxes, mix a small amount of clear furniture paste wax with a pinch or two of dark bronze dry artist's pigment. Wipe the tinted wax on the frame with a soft cloth, and let it stand for a few minutes. Wipe off the excess wax and polish the frame with a clean soft cloth.

2 | Use a sharp knife to cut the floral foam into slices ½" (1 cm)-thick. Arrange the foam pieces in a single layer on the floor of each shadow box, trimming it to fit. Glue the pieces in place using a low-temperature glue gun.

3 | Carefully trim the stems from the roses, leaving just enough so that the top of the flower head will be flush with the edge of the shadow box when the stem is inserted in the foam. Stand the roses upright in the foam to create a large heart outline, and glue in place. Use smaller roses to define the points and curves as needed.

4 | When the heart outline is complete, fill in the interior, placing the roses as close together as possible. Use roses of a different color to create a smaller heart within, if desired (see the shadow box at the left in the photo). If a rose is too large for a given space, strip off the outer petals one by one until it fits.

5 | Glue on roses of a different color to fill in the background around the heart, right up to the frame edges. Once again, strip away the outer petals as needed for a snug fit.

6 | Melt any "spiderwebs" of dried glue by aiming a hair dryer briefly over the entire shadow box.

BRANCHING OUT

Vary the dried flower selection to create new color and texture combinations. For example, use dried daisies, strawflowers, globe amaranth, or asters. Create other vivid graphic designs, such as Mondrian-inspired color blocks, circles, and stars, or even mimic a giant flower shape.

THE INSIDE DIRT

- Air-drying compromises the color of roses. Fresh red roses darken, yellow roses fade, and white roses discolor. To most effectively preserve the color, dry roses in silica gel.

- Test for dryness by gently squeezing the rosebud. If it feels soft in the center, allow more time to dry.

- Lightly apply hair spray or a hardening spray to discourage dried buds from crumbling.

BRANCHING OUT

Many objects lend themselves to crafting with whole pressed flowers. Try decorating picture frames, jewelry boxes, and lamp shades. Experiment with anemones, dogwood, primroses, hibiscus, bidens, and daisies. Hydrangea leaves, ferns, and Japanese maple leaves also create a pleasing effect.

THE INSIDE DIRT

• When petals overlap considerably, gently pluck the underlayer petals and press them separately. Then "rebuild" the flower by gluing the petals to the project one by one.

• Varnish will cause some colors to fade, so test it on a variety of pansies beforehand.

pressed pansy pots

Giant pansies put their best faces forward on these colorful painted pots. Choose a color palette that will both complement both your decor and show off the pansies.

MATERIALS

pressed giant pansies

terra-cotta pots

craft acrylic paint in blue, lavender, green, and white

white craft glue

satin water-based varnish

soft paintbrush

foam brushes

tweezers

clean, soft cloths

1 | Using a foam brush, apply a coat of satin water-based varnish to each pot, inside and out, as a sealer. Let dry.

2 | Paint each pot with two solid coats of blue, lavender, or green acrylic paint, letting dry completely after each coat.

3 | Mix one part white acrylic paint with one part water. Use a clean, soft cloth to apply this whitewash to each pot. Wipe around the pot in one direction, then use a slightly damp, clean section of the cloth to remove the excess whitewash where desired. Leave the rim of the pot in the solid color for contrast. Let dry.

4 | Use a soft paintbrush to apply white craft glue to the back of a giant pansy. Lift the pansy with tweezers and carefully place it on the pot surface. Press lightly with your fingertips to seal the petal edges. If the petals on your dried pansies have separated, glue them on one by one. Let dry.

5 | Apply four to six coats of satin water-based varnish to the outside of each pot, letting dry completely after each coat.

sewn seed-packet greeting cards

Give the gift of a garden by sending a greeting card complete with seeds. Use pressed flowers or petals from the same plant to provide a visual reference.

MATERIALS

pressed flowers and their corresponding seeds*

watercolor paper

purchased envelopes

sheer white organza

thread in desired color

sewing machine

scissors

*Marigolds and giant pansies are shown

1. Trim a sheet of watercolor paper and fold it with the grain to make a card that fits the purchased envelope.

2. Cut a rectangle of sheer organza at least 1" (3 cm) wider than the pressed flower, and twice as long as it is wide. Pull a few threads all around to fringe the edges.

3. Unfold the card, lay it flat, and center the organza rectangle on the front cover. Set the sewing machine to a long stitch length. Using matching or contrasting thread, machine-stitch along the bottom and two side edges of the organza, criss-crossing the stitching lines at the lower corners. Trim the threads.

4. Carefully fill the bottom half of the organza pocket with pressed flowers or petals. You may need to lightly shake the card or use a toothpick to force the flowers to the bottom. Stitch across the organza at the middle to seal the flowers in the fabric pocket. Fill the top half of the pocket with seeds, and stitch across the top of the organza to finish.

5. If desired, write the name of the flower across the bottom of the card, along with the date for season identification.

BRANCHING OUT

Create a see-through window by cutting a rectangle in the card front slightly smaller than the organza rectangle. Sew two pieces of organza to the card front, enclosing the pressed flower and seeds between them. Or, use this seed packet technique on scrapbook pages to make a heritage garden journal to hold seeds for the next growing season.

THE INSIDE DIRT

Generally, seeds should be stored in a cool, dry, dark location. To protect against moisture, place the seeds in paper envelopes and then place the envelopes inside plastic zipper-locked bags along with a sprinkling of silica gel. When stored properly, seeds potentially can keep for several years.

BRANCHING OUT

Modify the length and width of this runner
to design place mats, a square cloth lining
for a basket, or an extra-long runner to
drape across a bed. On larger pieces, try
using several wide ribbons for the flower
inserts. Play with different-sized ribbons
and flowers.

THE INSIDE DIRT

To coordinate the colors for this project,
choose and press your flowers first. Then
bring a sampling of the flowers with you
to the fabric store to pick out the ribbon
and fabric.

table runner with pressed flowers

Pressed flowers peek through a sheer ribbon on this easy-to-assemble table runner. No sewing machine is needed—the ribbons are bound in place with fusing tape and tiny, hand-embroidered stars. The pressed flowers are removable, which means you can display different selections from season to season or from year to year.

MATERIALS

assorted pressed flowers*	iron
2 yards (1.8 m) linen fabric	hand-sewing needle
2 yards (1.8 m) 2"-wide (5 cm) sheer ribbon	pins
2 yards (1.8 m) 1"-wide (3 cm) sheer ribbon	ruler
cotton sewing thread to match ribbon	scissors
narrow paper-backed fusing tape	*English daisies are shown

1. Gently wash and dry the linen fabric, and iron smooth. Cut a 72" x 17" (183 cm x 43 cm) rectangle from the fabric.

2. Fold and press the longer edges ½" (1 cm) and then 1" (3 cm) to the wrong side for a clean edge. Fuse the folded hem in place with fusing tape, following the manufacturer's instructions. For easier handling, cut the tape into short lengths for fusing.

3. Place the 2"-wide (5 cm) ribbon along the length of the runner, offsetting it 3" (8 cm) from one long edge, or as desired. Pin in place. Thread the needle with a double strand of thread. To tack the ribbon to the runner, embroider three over-lapping straight stitches in a star shape every 4" (10 cm) along both ribbon edges. Offset the stars from edge to edge so that they do not fall directly opposite each other. Tie off each design separately; do not carry the thread across the back of the runner.

4. Repeat step 2 to hem the short edges of the runner. Fold the hemmed section diagonally at the corners, for a mock miter, and hand-sew in place.

5. Cut the 1"-wide (3 cm) ribbon into four equal lengths. Place these ribbons, in pairs, across the width of the runner, about 8" (20 cm) in from each end and about ½" (1 cm) apart. Fuse down each edge, except where the ribbons cross the wider ribbon. Fold and fuse the ends to the wrong side of the runner.

6. Insert pressed flowers under the wider ribbon, interspersing them as desired.

flower tile mosaic jewelry box

Flower tiles are made by sandwiching desiccant-dried primroses between small glass squares, called "lights." The edges are sealed with copper foil tape. If you're not comfortable cutting the glass squares, have a glass and mirror shop do it for you.

MATERIALS

desiccant-dried primroses

unfinished wood jewelry box

1½" x 1½" (4 cm x 4 cm) glass tiles ("lights") cut from picture frame glass ¹⁄₁₆" (1 mm) thick*

¾" x ¾" (2 cm x 2 cm) vitreous glass tiles

copper foil tape

white sanded grout

craft acrylic paint in white and copper

clear-drying tile adhesive

V-notch trowel or flat-blade spreader

grout float

foam brush

small paintbrush

sponge

scissors

painter's low-tack masking tape

rubber gloves

spray glass cleaner

clean, soft cloths

paper towels

*Cut two glass lights for each flower tile desired

---

1. Arrange the clear and colored tiles on the jewelry box cover to plan the design, allowing approximately ¼" (5 mm) between tiles for the grout. (With sanded grout, this larger spacing is recommended; use latex grout if smaller spaces are desired.) Remove the tiles, keeping them in order.

2. Paint the jewelry box inside and out with two coats of white acrylic paint, letting dry after each coat. Load the small brush with copper paint. Paint a scroll accent across the front edge of the box in a loose and flowing stroke. Let dry.

3. Clean the glass lights with glass cleaner, and dry thoroughly. Snip the stem from a flower and center the flower on one square of glass. Place another glass square on top, making sure all the petals lie flat. Hold the glass squares together firmly and run a length of copper foil tape along one edge, burnishing it with your finger to seal. Continue applying the tape all around, burnishing and sealing as you go. When you reach the starting point, overlap and trim the tape at the corner. Press any overhanging tape onto the front and back surfaces of the glass. Wipe the tape with a soft cloth to remove any fingerprints. Repeat for each tile desired.

4. Apply tile adhesive to the jewelry box cover with a V-notch trowel or flat-blade spreader. Also brush adhesive on the back of each tile. Adhere the tiles to the jewelry box cover in the design mapped out in step 1. Let dry overnight.

5. Protect the glass flower tiles and the sides of the box with low-tack masking tape. Mix some white sanded grout with water following the manufacturer's instructions. Put on the rubber gloves. Apply the grout to the tiled surface with a grout float, angling it to force the grout in between the tiles. Let the grout set 15 minutes. Wipe the tiles with a clean, damp sponge, and wait another 10 minutes. Remove the masking tape. Clean the tiles with a damp cloth, and then polish them with a dry cloth to remove any remaining haze. Let cure according to the grout manufacturer's recommendations.

BRANCHING OUT

Use any pressed flowers, either singly or
in mini bouquets, to fill the glass tiles—
you can even use single leaves. For a
more random mosaic pattern, break the
tiles into smaller pieces with tile nippers,
as was done for the smaller yellow jewelry
box. The mosaic doesn't have to be grouted;
leaving the edges of the tiles exposed
adds sculptural interest.

THE INSIDE DIRT

• Whether you buy primroses for this
project or grow your own, avoid varieties with double blossoms. The multiple
layers of petals will not press well.

• To best preserve the color, dry your
primroses in silica gel. They will then
naturally press out between the glass
in this project.

BRANCHING OUT

It's difficult to varnish buttons without leaving behind sticky fingerprints or gumming up the holes. To make the job easier, build an inexpensive base from a large, thick piece of balsa wood and some toothpicks. Cut each toothpick in half and press the pointed ends into the balsa wood, side by side, using the button holes as a spacing guide. When you're ready to decoupage, simply push each button onto its toothpick holder—it will be held aloft, and you won't need to touch it while you work. As an added bonus, the toothpicks will keep the button holes clear of acrylic medium and varnish.

THE INSIDE DIRT

- Varnish can alter or fade the color of certain flowers, so it's always a good idea to test a few samples first.

- If fading does occur, you can use watercolors to reinforce or even change the flower color. Place the flower on a paper towel and lightly touch it up with water-thinned paint, brushing from the center outward. Let the paint dry completely before using the flower for crafting.

phlox button necklace

Pressed phlox flowers create a stylish statement on a button necklace. String a short necklace to wear as a choker, or a longer one for a more sophisticated look.

MATERIALS

pressed phlox flowers

13 to 18 large round buttons in peach, lavender, and green

black leather cord

2 small coil crimps

plated screw clasp

matte acrylic medium

satin water-based varnish

foam brushes

craft knife

jewelry pliers

1 | Using a foam brush, coat the surface of each button with matte acrylic medium. Place a pressed phlox flower on the damp surface, avoiding the button holes, if possible. Repeat for as many buttons as desired. Let dry completely.

2 | Apply one coat of satin water-based varnish to the surface of each button, and let dry. Use a sharp craft knife to carefully trim away any plant material covering the button holes.

3 | String flowered and plain buttons on the leather cord in a random sequence. Test-fit the strand periodically against your neck to determine the perfect length for your necklace.

4 | Fit a small coil crimp over each end of the cord, and pinch closed with pliers to secure. Separate the screw clasp into two pieces. Attach one piece to each end of the cord, using pliers to open and close the loops on the coil crimps.

polymer clay napkin rings

Bright and lively, these napkin rings are made by pressing fresh flowers into polymer clay.
The clay rings are then baked and glazed to keep the flowers' intense colors alive well past
the blooming season.

MATERIALS

assorted fresh flowers*

oven-hardening polymer clay

polymer clay glaze

rolling pin**

baking sheet**

craft knife

soft paintbrush

*Bidens, coreopsis, lobelia, and black-eyed Susan are shown

**Reserved for craft use

1 | Knead approximately two handfuls of polymer clay until it is smooth and easily workable. On a protected work surface, roll out the clay to a ¼" (5 mm) thickness.

2 | Use a craft knife to cut the clay into strips approximately 5" (13 cm) long x 1½" (4 cm) wide, or slightly narrower, if you prefer. Peel away and reserve the excess clay.

3 | Arrange fresh petals and flowers in a pleasing design on the middle of each clay strip. Press flowers firmly into the clay at the centers and around the edges to ensure that the botanicals stay embedded in the clay when it is manipulated.

4 | To shape the napkin ring, bring the ends of the strip together, flowers on the outside. Make sure the flowers remain pressed into the clay. Place each napkin ring flower side up on a cookie sheet. Repeat steps 1–4 to make additional rings, as desired.

5 | Follow the clay manufacturer's instructions to bake and cool the napkin rings. Check their progress at the earliest recommended time to prevent overbaking.

6 | Brush an even coat of polymer clay glaze on the front of each napkin ring, and let dry. Brush another coat of glaze on the bottom to complete the coverage, and let dry.

BRANCHING OUT

You can make beautiful flower tiles with polymer clay, or try jewelry such as pendants and earrings. Pierce a hole in the soft clay with a toothpick or nail to allow for chains and earring wires before oven-baking the finished design.

THE INSIDE DIRT

• Before making a complete set of napkin rings, bake a few sample pieces with your chosen flowers. That way, the exact baking time and temperature can be confirmed. Overbaking will cause the petals to curl inside their impressions.

• Use an oven thermometer while baking to make sure that the temperature is accurate.

• Testing will also let you discover which flowers, if any, do not work with this application. Some flowers change color dramatically when glaze is applied. Pink and red flowers, for instance, tend to brown.

BRANCHING OUT

Dried larkspur is a wonderful flower to use in interior floral arrangements. Its strong vertical appearance let's you experiment with height and dimension. You could change the levels of the different colors, or use them in smaller groups for a vibrant display.

THE INSIDE DIRT

• Larkspur air-dries beautifully. Simply hang it in small bunches in a warm, dark, dry location that has good air circulation.

• If you don't have access to a hydrangea bush, any sturdy leaf that has a firm vein structure can be substituted.

• If you are uncertain how much compound to use, make a few test prints on scrap wood first. A test print isn't absolutely necessary, however, as mistakes are easily sanded away when dry.

indoor window box

This colorful indoor window box can make it seem like summer all year long. The wooden box is relief-printed using a hydrangea leaf and joint compound, and the air-dried larkspur creates a thick hedge of color.

MATERIALS

air-dried larkspur*

fresh hydrangea leaf

unfinished wood box

dry floral foam

acrylic paint in off-white
and metallic peridot green

joint compound

spray matte acrylic varnish

scissors

foam brushes

soft, clean cloth

*We used three dried bunches each of dark pink
 and purple larkspur

1 Paint the unfinished box with one coat of off-white acrylic paint, brushing with the grain of the wood. Let dry.

2 Coat the back of a freshly picked hydrangea leaf with a thin layer of joint compound. Center the leaf, coated side down, on the front outside wall of the box, and press with your fingers to transfer the compound. Remove the leaf carefully. Print two more leaves, one on each side of the first print. Let dry completely.

3 Paint the entire box with another coat of off-white acrylic paint. Cover the leaves completely, but avoid filling in the relief details too heavily. Let dry.

4 Mix one part metallic green paint with one part water. Using a soft, clean cloth, apply the green mixture to the box in broad strokes along the wood grain. Wipe away the excess paint, leaving behind a soft wash of color. Add more color to the leaf shapes only, allowing the paint to collect in the detailed areas. Let dry. Spray with matte acrylic varnish to finish.

5 Pack the box tightly with dry floral foam, stopping 1" (3 cm) from the box rim. Sprinkle a light layer of dried larkspur leaves on the surface to prevent the foam from showing through the final arrangement. Starting at one end of the box, insert stems of dried pink larkspur into the foam, clipping them as needed to utilize the areas of fullest flowering. Pack the stems tightly next to each other and at the same height, for a solid, trimmed-hedge appearance. Change to purple larkspur at the middle, then finish with pink as shown. Add smaller stems to fill in around the perimeter where necessary for a full appearance.

woven lavender candle cuffs

Weave sweet-smelling air-dried lavender through wire-edged ribbon to make these decorative candle cuffs. The design is easily adapted to fit around candles of different sizes, from small glass votives to larger candle columns. Make certain that your votive is placed in a clear glass holder and that the lavender remains safely clear of the flame at all times.

MATERIALS

air-dried lavender	wire cutters
candle*	scissors
assorted wire-edged ribbons	hand-sewing needle
thread to match ribbons	low-tack painter's masking tape
fine-gauge copper wire or green florist's wire	*a votive candle in a clear glass holder and a thick column candle are shown
fabric glue	

1 Divide the lavender into 16 to 24 bunches of three stems each. Trim the stems to a uniform length that is appropriate for the candle height, as shown in the photo. To secure each bunch, wind fine-gauge wire twice around the stems, and clip off the excess.

2 Cut three to five 18" (46 cm) lengths of wired ribbon. Arrange the ribbons facedown on a flat surface, parallel to one another, leaving small spaces in between. Tape down the ribbons at one end with a piece of low-tack tape.

3 Weave the stems of one lavender bunch through the ribbons, over and under. Repeat with a second bunch, alternating the weaving pattern. Adjust the wire bindings so that they fall directly on a ribbon, not in between or under, so that they will not show on the right side. Continue weaving in bunches of lavender, pushing them tightly together as you go, until you have enough to encircle the votive holder or candle. To check the length, secure the open ribbon ends with painter's tape and gently wrap the weaving around the glass votive or candle to see if the ends meet. Add or remove bunches as needed, leaving an even number on the cuff, and retape the end.

4 Carefully wrap the weaving around the glass votive or candle, wire bindings on the inside, and bring the two taped ends together. Peel back the tape from the top ribbon on each side. Trim the ribbon ends so that they overlap about 1" (3 cm). Fold the top ribbon under for a neat finish, and join the overlap with a few drops of fabric glue. Reinforce the join by hand-tacking with needle and thread. Repeat to join the remaining ribbons. Retrim the bottom of the lavender stems if necessary, and double-check to make sure the wire wrappings are hidden.

BRANCHING OUT

Add other dried flowers, such as pink asters or orange strawflowers, to the ribbon area for a colorful accent. Simply glue them to the lavender weaving with a low-temperature glue gun. Or, use the ribbon and lavender weaving to cover a cylindrical lamp shade, accent a decorative birdhouse roof, or trim a picture frame.

THE INSIDE DIRT

• Harvest lavender at the base of its stem. It will dry well hanging in loose bunches.

• Lavender is covered in aromatic oil glands that emit a sweet, calming fragrance. It is also repellent to insects.

• In addition to the pale purple or "lavender" color for which the summer flowers on this evergreen perennial are best known, there are pink, blue, white, pale green, magenta, and deep purple blossoming varieties.

This chapter presents a variety of simple techniques for transferring botanical images onto everyday objects such as curtains, place mats, and pillows—giving them a stylish new identity. Whether you are looking to capture the intricate vein patterns in a leaf or the radiating petals of a flower, botanical imprints are a fabulous way to create memorable artistic images.

garden arts

As with all the crafts in this book, the projects are designed so that they are easy to make and open to variation, according to your tastes and available materials. Be sure to refer to "The Inside Dirt" for tips on finding supplies or making substitutions. Discover more project ideas that use the same techniques when you read "Branching Out." With a little ingenuity and creativity, you can make a variation on a project we show using materials you already have on hand. Or, you might use the techniques you learn here as a springboard to create something entirely unique.

BRANCHING OUT

Use the sun printing technique to illustrate
the pages or cover of a garden journal.
You can create a series of prints to frame,
or you might make specialty designs for a
decoupaged collage. Sun prints can also
be used for other paper-crafted items,
such as gift tags, greeting cards, and lamp
shades.

THE INSIDE DIRT

- For those who do not have a garden plot,
  fresh herbs will grow just as happily in
  containers and pots on a terrace or stoop.

- Before combining herbs in pots, check
  to make sure they require the same
  degree of sunlight, soil depth, and
  moisture.

herb sun-print clock

Paper tile cyanoprints decorate a clock that's perfect for a gardener's kitchen. Simply place sprigs of fresh herbs—parsley, sage, rosemary, and thyme—on the pretreated paper and place in bright sunlight to make the intense blue exposures.

MATERIALS

fresh parsley, sage, rosemary, and thyme

nine 4" x 4" (10 cm x 10 cm) squares of sun-print paper

12" x 12" (30 cm x 30 cm) unfinished clock face

clock works and hands

acrylic paint in white, dark blue, and light blue

all-purpose paste-glue or PVA glue

clear acetate or transparency paper

photocopier access or black fine-point permanent marker

foam brush

small artist's paintbrush

fine sandpaper

baking sheet

scissors

ruler

numeral templates (see pages 292–293)

1. Paint the clock face with two coats of white acrylic paint, letting dry after each coat. Paint the molded edge light blue, and let dry. Use a small paintbrush to add a fine line of dark blue paint at the join between the flat surface and the molding. Let dry. Lightly sand the molded edge to distress the paint.

2. Photocopy the clock numerals on pages 292–293 onto clear acetate or transparency paper (or use a black fine-point permanent marker to trace and color the numerals on acetate by hand). Cut out each acetate template on the cutting line.

3. Read the manufacturer's instructions for the sun-print paper. Bring the fresh herbs, numeral templates, unopened package of sun print paper, and baking sheet outside on a sunny day. Working quickly, open the sun-print paper and place nine squares blue side up on a baking sheet. Position the four numeral templates on top of four sheets, making sure that the template edges extend past the edges of the sun print squares. Lay fresh herbs on eight squares, including parsley on the square with the number 12, sage on number 3, rosemary on number 6, and thyme on number 9. Leave the ninth square empty.

4. Immediately expose the paper and herbs to bright sunlight until the paper turns white, typically 1 to 5 minutes, depending on the conditions. Bring the baking sheet indoors, remove the herbs and numerals, and rinse the paper under running water for 1 minute. Lay flat to dry. As the paper squares dry, the areas that were exposed to the light will turn a rich blue, revealing photographic prints of the herbs.

5. When the paper is completely dry, trim each piece to 3¼" x 3¼" (8 cm x 8 cm). Referring to the photo, arrange the paper tiles on a flat surface as they will appear on the clock face. Lay the top left tile facedown on a protected work surface, brush a very thin coat of all-purpose paste or PVA glue on the back, and position the tile on the clock face. Press firmly to seal, and carefully remove any oozing glue. Glue on the remaining tiles in the same way, allowing an even space in between as a faux grout line. Let dry.

6. Attach the clock works and hands as directed by manufacturer.

pear-print place mats

Pear trees always produce more fruit than you can eat! Use the excess produce to print these colorful, casual place mats, perfect for garden lunches or sunny breakfasts.

MATERIALS

purchased fabric place mats*

2 to 4 pears of different varieties

opaque fabric paint in brown, gold, green, red, and yellow

iron

knife

fine paintbrush

watercolor palette

triangular cosmetic sponges

spray water bottle

paper towel

*Include extra place mats or fabric for test prints

1 | Slice a pear in half from top to bottom, directly through the stem, if possible. Place each half, cut side down, on a paper towel for a few minutes to blot the juices.

2 | Pour a small amount of each of the opaque fabric paint colors onto the palette. Add a few drops of water to each color, and mix well.

3 | Use lightly dampened cosmetic sponges to load the flat cut surface of one pear half with paint. Begin by sponging yellow paint onto the entire surface. Add shading and detail with the gold, green, and red paints, using both the pear's natural skin coloring and the photograph as a guide. Apply the paint fairly heavily, to facilitate blending and printing. Color the edge and the stem with brown paint.

4 | Spray the painted surface lightly with water to blend the colors. Place the pear, painted side down, on the place mat. Press evenly and firmly on the entire pear, including the stem, to transfer the paint to the fabric. Lift the pear carefully to avoid smearing the print. You may want to do a few test prints on extra fabric before working on your final project.

5 | Repeat steps 3 and 4 to decorate all the place mats. If the stems don't print well, paint them in by hand using a fine brush and brown paint. Let dry overnight. Heat-set the paint by ironing on the reverse side of the fabric according to the paint manufacturer's instructions.

BRANCHING OUT

Instead of printing the pears in natural
colors, try something bold. Go for solid
bright colors in a grid pattern on primary
colored place mats, à la Andy Warhol.
Or, print pears on kitchen curtain valances
or trim. Other varieties of produce would
also make interesting prints: Try apples,
mushrooms, or any fruit or vegetable that
is fairly firm and has a distinctive shape.

THE INSIDE DIRT

• You don't have to have a pear tree growing in your yard for this project to be a
  success. Supermarket pears will work
  just fine. You'll find the greatest variety
  in the fall. The Bosc pear has a long,
  narrow taper to its neck. The Seckel
  pear is more rounded and petite.

• Use fruit that is firm, neither underripe nor
  overripe, and that has a well-developed
  core.

BRANCHING OUT

Create a strong and graphic design on the curtains by printing leaves in a repeating pattern or by using brightly colored fabric paint. Experiment with other fabric projects: plants with small leaves, such as fresh herbs, print more effectively onto proportionately smaller cloth items such as cotton napkins or a tea towel.

THE INSIDE DIRT

• Fresh leaves, not dried, work more effectively with this project. The vein structure is more prominent, making for a more detailed and interesting print.

• Each leaf can be reused about three to six times.

sheer leaf-print curtains

Beautiful, breezy, and fresh, these sophisticated white-on-white sheers are easy
to create with purchased curtain panels and a simple leaf printing technique.

MATERIALS

sheer white curtain panels

selection of fresh leaves with interesting shapes and strong vein patterns*

opaque white fabric paint

triangular cosmetic sponges

straight pins

scrap kraft paper or newsprint cut into squares slightly larger than the selected leaves

brayer

tweezers

iron

*Featured: ferns and hibiscus leaves

1 | Wash curtain panels according to manufacturer's directions to remove sizing. Press the curtains when dry, if necessary.

2 | Place one panel on a firm but protected work surface (a large sheet of heavy corrugated cardboard is perfect since the curtain panel can be secured flat with straight pins directly to the cardboard). Place a piece of scrap paper underneath the fabric exactly where you wish to make one leaf print.

3 | Place a leaf on a protected work surface. Dip a corner of a cosmetic sponge in the opaque white fabric paint. Dab the paint carefully on one side of the leaf, being careful to not overload the surface with paint. Note: results vary depending on which side of the leaf you use. Do at least one test print to see which side you prefer, and how much paint is appropriate for your design.

4 | Carefully place the leaf painted side down on the curtain. You may find tweezers helpful when handling the painted leaves. Cover the leaf with another piece of scrap paper, and roll over the leaf two to three times with a brayer using firm but not heavy pressure to transfer the paint to the curtain. To avoid smears, don't let the leaf shift while rolling. You may also find that using your hands to press the leaf into the fabric is a successful alternative to rolling with a brayer.

5 | Remove the protective scrap paper, and carefully lift the leaf from the fabric with tweezers. Let the paint set for a few minutes before proceeding. Repeat steps 2–5 as desired to cover the curtain panel with prints.

6 | When curtain is completely dry, heat-set the paint by ironing on the reverse side of the fabric according to paint manufacturer's instructions.

radish tiles

Use real radishes and polymer clay to make dimensional tiles for your home.
A reusable mold is made from the clay first, and multiple tiles can be pressed from it.

MATERIALS

fresh radishes with their leaves

1.75 lbs (795 g) oven-hardening polymer clay

craft acrylic paint in moss green or salmon

burnt umber acrylic paint

acrylic glaze base

spray matte acrylic varnish

rolling pin*

baking sheet*

wooden pointed sculpting tool

craft knife

foam brush

soft, clean cloth

*Reserved for craft use

1 | Knead half of the polymer clay until soft and workable. Roll it out on a baking sheet to make a slab ¾" (2 cm) thick and 6" x 6" (15 cm x 15 cm) square.

2 | Select, wash, and dry three radishes and three well-formed leaves. Arrange the leaves on the clay, overlapping them as desired. Press the edges of the leaves with your fingers to firmly imprint them into the clay. Position the radishes on the clay, matching up the cut stem ends to the leaves, and press firmly to make an impression. Remove the radishes and leaves and discard them. Emphasize the leaf shapes by lightly outlining them with a pointed wooden sculpting tool. Bake the clay mold and let it cool, following the manufacturer's directions.

3 | Knead half of the remaining polymer clay until soft and workable. Roll it out into a slab ½" (1 cm) thick and at least 5" x 5" (13 cm x 13 cm) square. Place the clay slab on the radish mold, covering the radishes but not completely covering the leaves. Press the soft clay into the mold, well into the radish forms. Peel the clay away from the mold, and place it, relief side up, on a baking sheet. Trim the edges with a craft knife to make a 4" x 4" (10 cm x 10 cm) square. Add an indented line border on the clean-cut edges with a wooden sculpting tool. Repeat with the remaining clay to make a second tile. Bake and cool the tiles according to the manufacturer's instructions.

4 | Apply a solid coat of moss green or salmon acrylic paint to each tile. Let dry. Mix one part burnt umber paint with one part acrylic glaze base. Brush the glaze mixture on the tile, letting it fill the indentations. Wipe away the excess, leaving behind dark accents to highlight the shapes and impart an aged look. Let dry. Spray with matte acrylic varnish.

BRANCHING OUT

You can make similar tiles with other firm fruits and vegetables. Try peas, beans, baby carrots, and cherries. Create a grouped wall hanging with your tiles, or mount them on found barn wood for a custom frame. You can also trim the clay into other shapes such as circles, rectangles, and hearts. Adhere hanging hardware with strong glue.

THE INSIDE DIRT

- Radishes are one of the first crops that can be sown in spring, usually as soon as the soil is workable. They grow relatively fast, some varieties maturing in as little as a few weeks.

- If you are using purchased radishes for this project, make sure the greens are still attached and fresh.

BRANCHING OUT

Any fabric project would be enhanced by an image transfer. Try this technique on place mats and tablecloths, scarves and aprons, curtains and fabric lamp shades. It also works on wax candles.

THE INSIDE DIRT

• Choose light-colored flowers. They will appear as white with gray detailing when photocopied. If the flower image is too dark, the color of the fabric will not show through the transfer.

• For crisp images, select flowers with readily identifiable shapes and large details.

• Arrange the flowers as flat as possible on the copier bed.

pop art pillows

Let your cut flowers live on as bright and modern pillows. All you have to do is transfer their photocopied images to fabric. The simple technique utilizes wintergreen essential oil to affix black copier toner to the fabric. The transferred images will withstand hand washing as long as a natural fiber fabric, such as cotton, is used for the backing.

MATERIALS

fresh flowers*

100% cotton twill fabric, 1 yard (.9 meter) each bright pink, yellow, and green

thread to match fabric

fiberfill

transparent fabric paint (optional)

wintergreen essential oil

photocopier access

sewing machine

iron

rotary cutter, cutting guide, and mat

scissors

straight pins

craft knife

burnishing tool or spoon

cotton balls

*Sunflower, gerbera daisy, and white lily are shown

1 | Wash and dry the fabric to remove any sizing, and iron flat.

2 | Place a fresh flower facedown on the photocopier bed, but do not close the lid. Make a photocopy with black toner, enlarging the image as desired. (Be sure to look away from the light during copying.) Adjust the lightness/darkness setting to make the background dark and the flower light for maximum contrast. Try several different settings until you get the best exposure.

3 | Use a craft knife and mat to cut out each flower. Cut a bit beyond the flower outline to create a dark, shadowy edge all around.

4 | Place the fabric right side up on a firm, protected work surface. Place the flower cutout on the fabric, toner side down, and secure with straight pins. Dip a cotton ball in wintergreen essential oil, and rub it over a small section of the photocopy until it is saturated. Go over the damp area with a burnishing tool or the back of a spoon, rubbing firmly to transfer the toner to the fabric. You can lift a corner of the photocopy to check the progress, but be careful to reposition it exactly. Continue transferring the image in sections, removing the straight pins when necessary. Let dry.

5 | To color the flower (if desired), use a foam brush to apply transparent fabric paint thinned with an equal amount of water. Test the results on scrap fabric first. If the paint is too watery, it will bleed beyond the transfer lines. If it is too thick, the black design will be hidden.

6 | Fold the fabric in a double layer, image transfer on top, and place on the cutting mat. Use the rotary cutter and guide to cut the desired pillow shape from both layers, allowing an extra ⅝" (2 cm) all around for the seam allowance. We cut a 26" x 12" (66 cm x 30 cm) rectangle, a 16" x 16" (41 cm x 41 cm) square, and an equilateral triangle with a 24" (61 cm) edge. You could also use a commercial pattern to cut the pillow shape.

7 | Place the two pillow pieces right sides together. Machine-stitch all around, making a ⅝" (2 cm) seam allowance; leave an opening on one side large enough for your hand to pass through. Clip the corners, turn right side out, and press the edges flat. Stitch ¼" (5 mm) from the edges all around, except at the opening. Stuff the pillow with fiberfill, placing it evenly throughout. Continue the stitching line to close the opening.

sun print hatboxes

Turn plain cotton fabric into a custom-designed botanical print. Simply treat the fabric with a special paint, lay the dried botanicals on top, and expose to the sunlight. Glue your newly printed fabrics around hatboxes to hold seed packets, crafting supplies, or photos of your garden.

MATERIALS

pressed botanicals*

3 papier-mâché circular boxes

white 100% cotton broadcloth

Pebeo Setacolor transparent fabric paints in Buttercup, Parma Violet, Moss Green, and Pernod Yellow

acrylic paint in white, yellow-gold, moss green, and purple

wide ribbon in coordinating colors

matte decoupage medium

spray adhesive

spray matte acrylic varnish

iron

scissors

straight pins

foam brushes

disposable cups for mixing paint

sheet of heavy-duty cardboard

large plastic garbage bag

*Hydrangea blossoms, Japanese maple leaves, and Queen Anne's lace are shown

1 | Machine-wash the cotton fabric to remove size. Dry and iron smooth. Rough-cut rectangles of fabric large enough to cover the sides of each of your chosen boxes, with some overlap on all sides.

2 | Mix the Buttercup and Parma Violet fabric paints with an equal amount of water, each in its own disposable cup. To obtain the green shade, mix equal parts of Moss Green and Pernod Yellow, and then mix in the water.

3 | Cover the heavy-duty cardboard with the large plastic garbage bag to make a protected, transportable work surface. Lay the fabric pieces on top. Spray or sponge the fabric with water to seal it to the work surface.

4 | Using foam brushes, apply the three diluted paints from step 2 to the three fabrics (one color per fabric) in smooth, broad strokes. Working quickly, place the pressed botanicals on the fabrics and press down firmly so they are secure. Bring the entire board into the sun. Wait 15 minutes, and then check the exposure by carefully lifting a corner of one botanical. When fully exposed (15 minutes to 1 hour), bring the entire board inside, remove the botanicals, and allow the fabric to finish air-drying. Iron the fabric for 2 to 3 minutes on the cotton setting to fix the paint.

5 | Apply one coat of white acrylic paint to each box. Let dry. Apply a coat of decoupage medium to the outside of one box with a foam brush. Carefully place the corresponding fabric piece on the wet medium, smoothing it carefully with your fingers. Overlap the ends, and leave some fabric overhanging at the top and bottom. Fold the excess at the bottom to the underside of the box, and glue down firmly with decoupage medium. Turn the excess at the top to the inside of the box, and glue in place. Glue a length of wide contrasting ribbon around the inside rim to conceal the raw fabric edges.

6 | Paint the box covers with acrylic paint to match the fabric, and let dry. Apply a wash of diluted white acrylic paint with a soft cloth, wipe off the excess, and let dry. Glue pressed botanicals to the cover with spray adhesive. Seal with a coat of spray matte acrylic varnish.

BRANCHING OUT

You can paint fabric in a wash of stripes
and cloudy textures by brushing on one
color first, leaving some areas white, and
then filling the blank areas with another
color. The diluted paints will bleed into
each other, creating a soft yet vibrant
effect. Use this fabric decoupage technique to make a journal cover, lamp shade,
or picture frame. Or, use the finished fabric
to create scarves, pillows, table linens,
curtains, or patchwork quilts.

THE INSIDE DIRT

• Botanicals with distinct, recognizable
  shapes work best for this project.

• When pressing botanicals, make sure
  neither the petals nor the leaves overlap.
  Overlapping plant material will take
  away from the shape definition that is
  so effective with sun printing.

• Remember to press materials of like size
  and substance on the same sheet so that
  they dry at the same rate.

BRANCHING OUT

Try this decoupage technique on any wood surface. At most craft shops, you'll find a large selection of unfinished wood products, including frames, shelves, storage boxes, and cabinets. Instead of seed packets, use cutout words and images from flower and seed catalogs (arrange them in a collage) or color photocopies of botanical drawings from books.

THE INSIDE DIRT

• If a seed packet you want to use for this project still contains seeds, save them in a paper envelope (one type of seed per envelope). Be sure to label the type of seed and the date purchased on the paper envelope.

• Seal the paper envelopes in a plastic, zipper-locked bag along with a few grains of silica gel.

• Properly stored seeds can potentially keep for several years.

seed packet tea tray

Recycle colorful seed packages by gluing them onto a tea tray. This decoupage technique utilizes acrylic matte medium—a liquid easily found in craft and art supply stores—to glue and seal the paper to the wood surface.

MATERIALS

empty seed packets*

unfinished wood tea tray*

four basswood strips, each
24" x ¼" x ¼" (61 cm x 5 mm x 5 mm)

teak water-based stain

dark green acrylic paint

acrylic matte medium

satin water-based varnish

wood glue

craft knife, plus saw blade

straightedge

cutting mat

foam brushes

clean, soft cloth

*A 12" x 18" (30 cm x 46 cm) tray covered with 18 packets is shown

1 | Remove the hardware, if any, from the tea tray. Apply teak water-based stain to the surface with soft cloth, following the manufacturer's directions. Let dry.

2 | Trim off all four edges of each seed packet, using a craft knife, straightedge, and cutting mat. Save the front panel of each packet.

3 | Place one panel facedown on a protected work surface. Using a foam brush, apply acrylic matte medium to the back of the panel. Position the panel, glue side down, in one corner of the tray, and smooth in place. Repeat to adhere the remaining panels in a brickwork pattern, overlapping the edges slightly. Trim the last few panels as needed to fill out the edges. Apply a final thin layer of matte medium to the entire surface, and let dry.

4 | Attach the saw blade to the craft knife. Cut the four basswood strips to size to line the inside edges of the tray floor, butting the ends at the corners. Paint the strips dark green, and let dry. Apply wood glue to two adjoining faces of each strip, and glue in place.

5 | Apply three to four light coats of water-based varnish to the entire tray, letting dry after each coat. When completely dry, reattach the hardware.

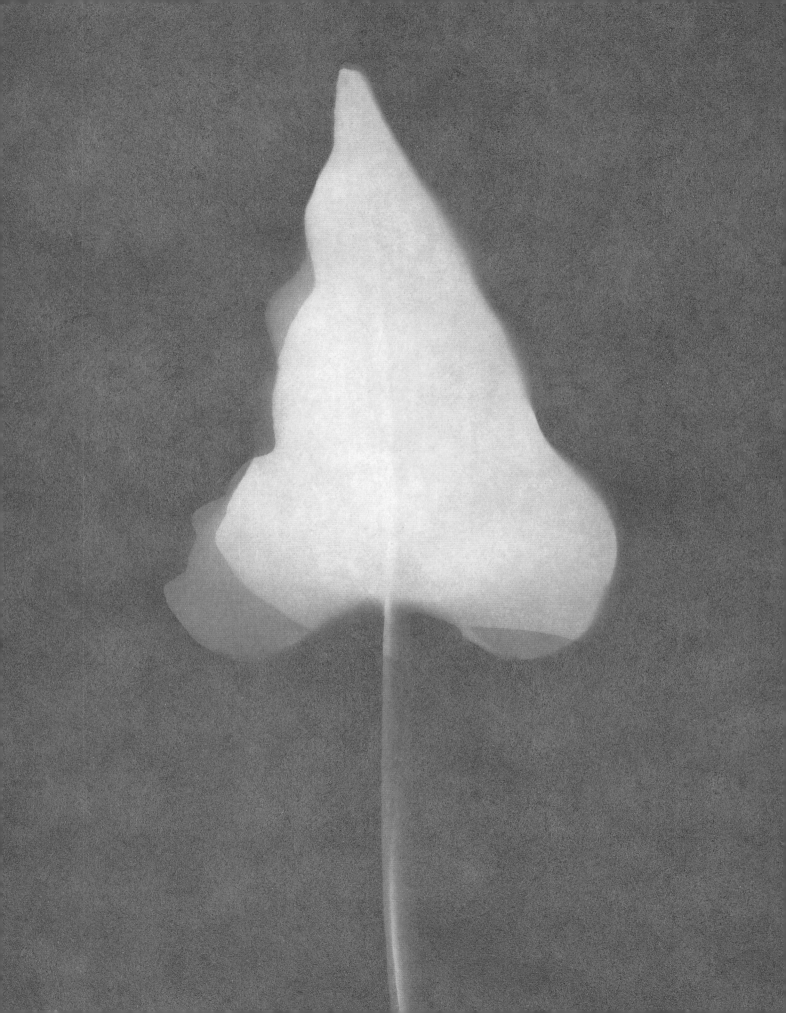

The garden is well known as a place that rejuvenates the body as well as the soul. This chapter explores various ways to pursue this end. Botanicals are used to make simple projects intended for self-care or quiet moments of relaxation. From bath teas to sachets to soaps, this chapter in particular integrates aromatherapy with garden-inspired crafts. You'll find instructions for bath teas that take just minutes to make but can help take you miles away from your worries.

the garden spa

A bolster wrapped in candy-striped silk will certainly add an elegant touch to the head of a bed or end of a sofa. What is not so apparent is that the pillow is lined with crumpled, dried sage, the essential oils of which are said to inspire sweet dreams and rest. If anything, the crafts in this chapter are meant to remind us to stop and smell the roses—and anything else in the garden that prompts us to take a refreshing pause.

herbal-blend bath teas

In the dead of winter, the gentle aromas of homemade bath teas will bring your garden back to life. These bath tea pouches are made with inexpensive cheesecloth, so you needn't feel guilty about discarding the cloth after a few uses. As you prepare new pouches, you can reuse the ribbon and button tie. Hang the bag from your tub spout, or let it float freely in the bath water.

MATERIALS

tea blend of dried herbs and flowers*

cheesecloth

¼" (5 mm) sheer ribbon

vintage shank-style buttons

large-eyed needle

scissors

*See "Branching Out" for suggested blends

1 | Fold the cheesecloth in a double layer. Cut through both layers, making an 8" (20 cm) square. Pour approximately ½ cup (.125 l) of the tea blend into the center of the cheesecloth square.

2 | Cut a 32" (81 cm) length of sheer ribbon, trimming the ends diagonally to prevent fraying. Fold the ribbon in half, and tie an overhand knot at the middle of this shortened length. The large loop that is formed can be used to hang the bag on the tub spout.

3 | Draw up and cinch all four corners of the cheesecloth with your fingers to create a pouch around the tea mix. To secure the pouch, place the knotted portion of the ribbon firmly against it and wrap the loose ends of the ribbon several times around in opposite directions. Tie once, without knotting. Thread the ribbon ends through the button shank, using the needle if necessary. Retrim the ribbon ends.

BRANCHING OUT

The following is a sampling of some of the herbs and flowers you might wish to use in homemade bath teas. They are categorized according to the effect their aromas tend to induce.

Soothing
lavender

chamomile

rose petals

lemon verbena

bergamot

Invigorating or refreshing
rosemary

jasmine

mint

rose geranium

Pleasing
lemon balm

pineapple sage

lemon verbena

mints

rosemary

scented geranium leaves

chamomile buds

sweet woodruff

lavender

bee balm

Muscle-relaxing
sage

rose

strawberry leaves

comfrey

rosemary

lavender

To add bright color accents
calendula

violets

nasturtium

THE INSIDE DIRT

• Screen-drying is the ideal way to pre-pare herbs and flowers for bath teas.

• If you are drying large quantities, use several screens and stack them on tin cans of equal size. This will save space but still allow ample air circulation.

• Store dried bath tea ingredients individ-ually or in blends in airtight containers.

• If the water from your tub spigot does not run very hot, make a concentrated bath brew. Heat a kettle of water on the stove until boiling. Place the bath tea pouch in a saucepan, pour in the boiling water, and let it steep a few minutes. Transfer the steaming concentrate to fresh bath water.

BRANCHING OUT

The essential oils of many herbs and flowers have distinct therapeutic effects, such as being relaxing or invigorating. See page 237 for a short list of herbs and their corresponding characteristics. For further information on this topic, refer to books on aromatherapy and herbal medicine.

THE INSIDE DIRT

- Use clear glycerin soaps if you want the botanical you are adding to be readily visible.

- Dried calendula, hibiscus, and rose hips retain their color well in these soaps. Most herbs, unfortunately, turn brownish in color.

- Always use dried botanicals when adding to soaps. Fresh botanicals can present bacterial problems.

real simple garden soaps

"Melt-and-pour" glycerin soaps let you make your own soaps without having to work with lye. You simply melt glycerin soap bases, pour the liquid into molds along with your favorite garden flower or herb, and wait a brief period for the soaps to harden. For these soaps, olive oil clear glycerin soap base and honey glycerin soap base were used in alternating layers with black-eyed Susans suspended in between.

MATERIALS

dried herbs, flower petals, or whole flowers

"melt-and-pour" glycerin soap

one essential oil, or more, of choice

soap molds or plastic containers

medium-sized saucepan

heatproof bowl and cover*

stainless steel spoon

*Choose a bowl that fits on the rim of the saucepan

1 Fill the saucepan about 2" (5 cm) deep with water, and bring to a gentle simmer. Set the heatproof bowl on top, making sure it does not touch the simmering water.

2 Add the soap to the heatproof bowl. Cover and let melt, stirring occasionally. Once fully melted, remove the bowl from the pan. Let cool slightly, about 2 minutes.

3 Stir in .5 to .7 ounces (14 to 20 g) of essential oil per 1 pound (457 g) of soap. If using petals or herbs that will be evenly distributed in the soap, stir them in along with the oil. Pour the liquid soap into the molds. Let sit until the soaps have firmed up.

4 To suspend a single flower or other botanical in the center of the soap, fill the mold only one-quarter to one-third full and let harden about 20 minutes. Then add the flower, followed by more soap mixture. (To make the soaps shown here, we added olive oil–based soap and honey-based soap in four alternating layers.) Let sit until the soaps have firmed up.

sage-lined bolster

The mellow aroma of common sage is known to have soothing, sleep-inducing effects—
perfect on a restless night or to encourage an afternoon nap. The sage in this bolster
is hidden from view, encased in a muslin liner, but its gentle aroma will nonetheless find
its way to your senses. When the essential oils in the sage dissipate, the liner can be
removed and replenished with freshly dried sage from a new season.

MATERIALS

dried and crumbled sage

striped fabric for pillow cover*

muslin or other natural cotton fabric*

ribbon to match pillow cover fabric*

thread to match pillow cover fabric

bolster form (in desired size)

sewing machine

scissors

hand-sewing needle

straight pins

tape measure

*Purchase sufficient fabric and ribbon for your size bolster

1 | Measure the length and circumference of the bolster, and add 2" (5 cm) to each measurement. Cut two rectangles to
these dimensions from muslin. Set the sewing machine to a short stitch length. Machine-stitch the rectangles together
around three sides with a ⅝" (2 cm) seam allowance, leaving one of the "length" sides open. Clip the corners diagonally, turn right side out, and press. Loosely fill the muslin pocket with dried crumbled sage. Close the open edge by whip-
stitching by hand.

2 | Bring the two "length" edges of the liner together, overlapping them slightly to form a tube, and whipstitch by hand. Pull
the tube over the bolster. Adjust the sage filling so that it is evenly distributed around the bolster.

3 | Remeasure the pillow length and circumference and add 1½" (4 cm) to each measurement. (With the added liner, the cir-
cumference should measure slightly larger than in step 1.) Referring to the diagram on page 294, cut one center panel
rectangle to the new dimensions from striped fabric, stripes running parallel to the "circumference" edges. Cut two side
panels with the stripes running the opposite way, making each panel at least twice as wide as the bolster diameter, or
so that the ends can be folded and cinched.

4 | Fold each side panel in half lengthwise, right side out, as indicated in the diagram. Press to set the crease. Pin the long
raw edges to the center panel, right sides together. Machine-stitch, making a ⅝" (2 cm) seam allowance. Press the seam
allowances toward the center panel. Fold the entire piece in half lengthwise, right sides together, and stitch the longer
edges together to form a tube. Press the seam open. Turn right side out.

5 | Gently insert the bolster into the striped tube covering until it is centered. Cinch the end panels with your fingers and
tie with ribbon.

BRANCHING OUT

All shapes and sizes of pillows can be used for this project. The choice in fabric is virtually limitless. Do be sure, however, to use a natural-fiber fabric that breathes so that the aroma of the sage can be effectively diffused.

THE INSIDE DIRT

• Harvest sage foliage when it is perfectly mature, neither immature nor too old, to obtain peak levels of essential oils.

• Dry sage leaves on a screen or other surface that allows air to circulate, and be sure to place the screen in a dark, dry location.

• Sage is fully dry when it breaks crisply and crumbles readily.

BRANCHING OUT

Combine different colored fillings to change your decorating scheme quickly and easily. For a stronger visual effect, fill or top off one section with a single whole dried flower. Or, cover the petals and grains with a secure piece of glass, and turn the shadow box back into a wall-mounted display filled with home-spun items and colorful art.

THE INSIDE DIRT

- To make a simple, homemade potpourri, place dried petals, herbs, leaves, seeds, and spices in an airtight container. Place the container in a dark, dry, and relatively warm place. Store this way up to two months, turning the jar periodically to blend the contents.

- If a potpourri aroma fades or is faint from the start, revive it with a small piece of paper dabbed with essential oil. Add the paper to the jar and then reseal the jar.

petal potpourri tea-light holder

A purchased shadow box becomes an enchanting holder for deconstructed potpourri
and colorful grains, simply by adding dividers made of balsa wood. A faux zinc finish adds
an urban accent to the finished craft. Tea lights held in metal cups protect the potpourri
from the open flames, but even so, do not leave the burning candles unattended.

MATERIALS

assorted botanicals*

unfinished wood shadow box

balsa wood strips (the width should match
the box depth)

three tea lights

essential oil for the dried flower petals,
if desired

warm charcoal gray acrylic paint

silver metallic dry artist's pigment

clear paste furniture wax

clean, soft cloth

craft knife with fine saw blade

cutting mat

foam brush

*Air-dried rose petals, popcorn kernels, and soybeans
are shown

1. Cut three balsa wood strips, one the length of the inside box and two the width of the inside box. Mark each short piece at the midpoint. Mark the longer piece in thirds. Cut a notch at each mark, stopping halfway through the strip. Test-fit the balsa wood strips by interlocking the short pieces to the long piece at the notches. Trim the notches as needed until the pieces fit together.

2. Paint the shadow box and balsa wood strips with two coats of warm charcoal gray acrylic paint, letting dry after each coat.

3. Tint some clear paste furniture wax by mixing in a small amount of silver metallic dry artist's pigment. Wipe the wax onto the painted box and balsa wood with a clean, soft cloth. Remove any excess wax, and let dry. Buff with a clean cloth to a soft sheen.

4. Assemble the painted balsa wood strips to make the inside dividers. Place the assembly into the shadow box. Fill the sections with selected dried petals and grains, and add tea lights where desired.

no-sew organza sachets

These sachets just might be too pretty to hide away in a drawer or a closet. Made of metallic organza, frayed silk dupioni trim, and button or beaded accents, they pay a nod to modern elegance as well as a little well-deserved indulgence. All of the pieces are joined with fusing tape, making it easy to make up multiples for gifts. The fusing tape also helps prevent the sheer organza from fraying at the seams.

MATERIALS

dried flower petals, herbs, or potpourri

metallic organza fabric

matching metallic silk dupioni fabric

buttons, beads, or other small accents

thread

⅝"-wide (2 cm) paper-backed fusing tape

iron

hand-sewing needle

1 Cut an 8½" x 15" (22 cm x 38 cm) rectangle from the sheer organza fabric. Fold it in half crosswise to make a pocket, and press to set the crease. Fuse the side edges together, following the fusing tape manufacturer's instructions and placing the tape ¼" (5 mm) in from the edges. After fusing, trim the sides even with the outer tape edge to make an 8" x 7½" (20 cm x 19 cm) pocket.

2 Cut a 9½" x 4" (24 cm x 10 cm) rectangle from the metallic silk dupioni, so the nub runs parallel to the longer edges. Referring to the diagram on page 295, fold the rectangle in half, wrong side in, and press to set the crease. Open up the rectangle. Fold and press each short edge ¾" (2 cm) to the wrong side for the flaps. Pull out a few threads along both long edges to create a fringed effect.

3 Lay the silk dupioni wrong side up on the ironing surface. Following the diagram, cut and fuse tapes 1, 2, and 3 in position on section A. Let cool. Peel off the paper backing. Position the open end of the organza pocket over section A, aligning the raw edges on the fold. Fuse in place, and let cool. Next, cut and fuse tapes 4 and 5 to the flaps, and let cool. Peel off the paper backing, fold in the flaps, and fuse in place.

4 Place a modest amount of dried petals, herbs, or potpourri in the sheer pocket. Fuse tape 6 in position on section B, overlapping the flaps, and let cool. Peel off the paper backing. Fold section B down onto section A, enclosing the top of the sheer pocket, and fuse in place. (Be sure to push sachet contents to the pocket bottom, out of the way of the iron.) Embellish by sewing on accent buttons or beads.

BRANCHING OUT

To make a drawstring-style sachet for hanging, follow the same technique to make the sheer pocket. Then fold in the top edge by about 1¼" (3 cm) and fuse in place to form a casing. Thread a ribbon through the casing and cinch closed to create a purse effect. Embellish with beads at the ribbon ends or attach a beaded fringe along the sachet base.

THE INSIDE DIRT

• To fill sachets, use dried petals from your favorite fragrant flower, an air-dried insect-repellent herb, such as lavender, or a potpourri of flowers and herbs.

• Regardless of the filler chosen, you may want to boost the fragrance with a few drops of an essential oil. Choose an oil-bearing scent of an ingredient in your potpourri mix or a scent that complements your dried flowers or herbs.

BRANCHING OUT

If you prefer to make a larger votive, use proportionately larger flowers. This is also a great way to capture the bright colors of autumn leaves.

THE INSIDE DIRT

- Choose petite yet bold flowers with very little overlapping of petals. The flowers must be pressed well to avoid air pockets in the design.

- If using leaves, do not let them dry to the point of brittleness, or they will crackle when they are molded around the votive.

- Fibrous rice paper tears more easily if you crease it first. Run your fingernail or the handle of a spoon along the fold line to set the crease.

petite botanical votive set

On each of these small, narrow votives, a single pressed flower is muted by a layer of translucent rice paper. The edges of the paper are torn and stop short of the votive rim and base for a soft, organic look. Aside from the time it takes for the glue to dry, this project requires just fifteen minutes of hands-on attention.

MATERIALS

pressed flowers*

3 glass votives with candles

translucent rice paper

decoupage glue

foam brush

steel cork-backed ruler

spray glass cleaner

paper towels

*Coreopsis is shown

1. Lay the paper on a flat surface. Place the steel ruler on top, hold it down firmly, and tear the paper by drawing it up along the ruler edge. Use this method to tear a rectangle for each votive, large enough to wrap around once and overlap by at least ¼" (5 mm). Make the height of the rectangle slightly less than the votive, to show a bit of the glass rim and base.

2. Remove the candles, and clean and dry the glass votives. Using the foam brush, apply a thin, even coat of decoupage glue to the glass at the spot where the flower will be placed. Carefully position the flower on the glass, making sure there are no wrinkles or air bubbles in the petals. Let dry in place.

3. Gently apply a thin, even coat of glue to the glass votive where the paper will be applied. Starting at the back, position the edge of the paper on the glass, then slowly wrap the paper around, smoothing out any wrinkles and air pockets as you go. Apply another thin, even coat of glue over the paper. Let dry overnight.

flower waters in etched bottles

Lightly fragranced waters in etched bottles add a personal accent to your home spa decor. Etching is much simpler than you might think, but do be sure to wear protective gloves and eyewear when using the highly caustic etching cream.

MATERIALS

rose or lavender water (see page 249)

glass bottles with cork stoppers

etching cream

craft knife

self-adhesive shelf lining paper

carbon transfer paper and pen

rubbing alcohol

cotton swab

foam brush

rubber gloves

protective eyewear

etching patterns (page 296)

1   Remove the stoppers from the bottles, wash the bottles, and let air-dry completely.

2   Cut a 3" x 3" (8 cm x 8 cm) square of self-adhesive shelf lining paper. Transfer one of the etching patterns from page 296 to the center of the paper with transfer paper and a pen.

3   Remove the backing from the shelf paper. Press the paper, adhesive side down, on the glass bottle, so that the design is well positioned on the bottle's surface. Cut out the design carefully with a craft knife. Peel off the cutout sections of the design to be etched.

4   Burnish the remaining pieces of the design firmly onto the glass with your fingernail. Clean the exposed glass area with a cotton swab dipped in rubbing alcohol, and let dry.

5   Wearing protective clothing as recommended by the manufacturer, use a foam brush to apply a thick, even coat of etching cream to the exposed areas of the design. Keep the cream from touching any glass on the perimeter of the shelf paper. Let sit as recommended, usually from 5 to 12 minutes. Rinse the cream completely from the bottle, remove the shelf paper mask, and let the bottle dry to reveal the etched design.

6   Repeat steps 2–5 for each bottle. Fill the finished bottles with flower waters and replace the cork stoppers.

THE INSIDE DIRT

- If rose or lavender is not your fragrance of choice, there remains a wide choice of other flowers and essential oils that you can use alone or in combination to make floral or herb-scented waters.

- As with perfume, consider the characteristics of a flower, herb, or essential oil. Seek balance, combining an aroma that is stimulating with one that is calming and then punctuating the two with a strong middle note, something decidedly in between.

RECIPES

For rose water:
- 1 cup (.25 liter) packed fresh deep red rose petals (approximately 6 large garden roses)
- 2 cups (.5 liter) boiling distilled water
- ¼ cup (.06 liter) vodka
- few drops of rose essential oil (optional)

For lavender water:
- ½ cup (.125 liter) dried lavender
- 1 cup (.25 liter) boiling distilled water
- ¼ cup (.06 liter) vodka
- few drops of lavender essential oil (optional)

Place the lavender or rose petals in a clean, sterilized glass container. Pour the boiling distilled water over the botanicals. Add the vodka, seal, and let steep for one week. Strain the waters, add essential oil if desired, and funnel into decorative bottles.

Just as a garden is about vitality and vibrance, it is also about stillness and peace. The projects in this chapter reflect the Zen-like aspect of natural objects. From a mirror framed with sand and garden pebbles to an Asian-influenced money plant lamp shade, each project assumes a simple, understated approach.

from the zen garden

Of all the chapters, this one works with the greatest variety of materials and perhaps the most eccentric. The delicate dry, outer skins of garlic and onions are used to make tiny bowls. A Zen centerpiece is assembled from river stones, Spanish moss, and strawflowers. They are the type of projects that inspire the imagination as well as instruct the mind. Consider what materials you have readily available and how you might adapt and modify a project in order to make use of them. That way, instead of waiting to craft later, you can begin in the Zen now.

BRANCHING OUT

This mosaic technique is a perfect decoration for memento and jewelry boxes or clock faces. You can also use it to accent backsplashes, table tops, headboards, or even a chair rail in a beach house.

pebbles and sand mirror

Even the pesky pebbles from your garden can be put to good use in this Zen garden–inspired frame. A mixture of tile adhesive and craft sand makes a textured grout that will hold your found pebbles securely in place.

MATERIALS

collection of pebbles

unfinished wood frame with a flat surface molding

dyed desert craft sand in tan, dark brown, and natural

burnt umber acrylic paint

hanging hardware

clear-drying mosaic tile adhesive

clear furniture paste wax

putty knife

foam brush

measuring cup

clean, soft cloth

large disposable container and stirrer

1. Paint the frame with the burnt umber acrylic paint, and let dry. Add hanging hardware to the back of the frame, if desired.

2. For a large frame (cut the following recipe in half for a small frame), combine ½ cup (.125 liter) natural craft sand with ¼ cup (.06 liter) each dark brown and tan sand. Place the combined sands, 1 cup (.25 liter) clear-drying tile adhesive, and a large spoonful of water in a disposable container, and mix well. Add more sand, adhesive, or water as necessary to make a smooth, thick, spreadable mixture. The texture and consistency should resemble creamy peanut butter.

3. Prop the frame, right side up and level, on some old jars or cans over a protected work surface. Spread the sand mixture evenly over the front and sides of the frame with a putty knife. The mixture will self-level and maintain a smooth surface on the top, but you may need to even out and reapply the sides manually a few times.

4. When the frame is completely covered, let the sand mixture set for 10 minutes. Scrape any drips off the bottom edges as they occur.

5. Set the pebbles firmly into the sand mixture. Let dry completely. Dip a clean cloth in furniture wax and lightly wipe the pebbles to accentuate their colors and provide a protective finish.

garlic skin bowls

In a technique resembling papier-mâché, garlic skins are layered and overlapped to make delicate bowls, perfect for storing potpourri, small beads, or specialty salts, such as those shown here. The skins were curled back at their tips to create the blossomlike appearance. The process is meditative, and no two bowls look alike.

MATERIALS

several bulbs of garlic*

PVA glue (neutral pH adhesive)

spray varnish

craft knife

small, sharp scissors

small soft paintbrush

disposable plastic container

aluminum foil

*Red onion skin bowls also shown here

1. Use a craft knife to cut through the dry, delicate outer skin of the garlic bulb, starting at the base and working toward the tip. If possible, run the blade between the two cloves of garlic that lie underneath. Make three or four cuts around the head so that you can peel off the outer skin in large pieces. Carefully slice them free from the base and set them aside. The remainder of the garlic can be used for cooking.

2. Crumple and wad the foil into a small ball the size of a finished bowl. For garlic skin bowls, 1½" to 2" (4 cm to 5 cm) in diameter is ideal. Flatten one side of the ball slightly, so that it will sit on the work surface without rolling.

3. In a disposable plastic container, dilute some glue with three times as much water. Sit the foil ball on a protected work surface. Place one piece of garlic skin over the top of the ball, letting it drape down one side. Lightly brush the end near the top with diluted glue. Place another layer of skin on top of the ball, draping it toward the opposite side. Repeat to cover the entire ball, brushing glue wherever the papery skins overlap.

4. When the skins have dried enough to hold their place, remove the foil ball. Curl back the tips of the skins to create a blossom effect, if desired. Let dry completely. Apply spray varnish. If the bowl will be used to hold salt or any kind of food, be sure to use a food-safe varnish.

BRANCHING OUT

Try adhering small pressed flowers to the outside or inside of garlic or onion skin bowls. Or, use flower petals instead of the skins to make the bowls. Dry the petals partially, not all the way. If they are fully dried, they will be too crisp to mold around the foil ball. Leaves are another possibility.

THE INSIDE DIRT

• If you purchase garlic or onions to make this project, look for clean, thick, unblemished skins. Use the dry outer layers only. The waxy interior layers, particularly of onions, do not take to the glue and are apt to decompose.

• If you are growing your own garlic, try varieties with red or purple-tinted skin for this project. Elephant varieties have cloves that are large and distinct, which makes the outer skins somewhat easier to release.

• Collect garlic and onion skins over time, as you do your routine cooking. Store the collected skins in a shoe box or other protective container until you are ready to use them.

BRANCHING OUT

Texture is the key to filling this centerpiece.
You can also use landscaping stones, cedar,
or other ornamental garden fills. Instead of
using a shadow box, fill separate matching
elements, such as four soy sauce dishes,
four rice bowls, or four decorative ashtrays.
Protected tea lights could be added, but
make sure to supervise their burning.

THE INSIDE DIRT

• Strawflowers and other "everlasting"
  flowers can be found year-round in the
  dried flower section of most craft stores.

• If you grow your own strawflowers, harvest them when the buds just begin to
  bloom. They will open further as they dry.

• The stems on strawflowers weaken as
  they dry. If you wish to maintain the
  stems, support the flowers on a mesh
  screen, letting the stems dangle underneath so that they aren't crushed.

zen-inspired centerpiece

Turn a shadow box into an Asian-inspired centerpiece by filling it with items of distinctive texture. Polished stones, gravel, bamboo, and moss combine for a "four seasons" theme, and dried strawflowers float on the surface, like water lilies on a calm pond.

MATERIALS

finished wood shadow box

polished river stones

marble river gravel

bamboo

Spanish moss

air-dried strawflowers

dry floral foam

craft knife with fine saw blade

cutting mat

ruler

1. Cut the floral foam to fill the shadow box, stopping 1" (3 cm) from the rim. Mark the foam surface into four equal quadrants. Cut away the foam in one quadrant to half its thickness. Reserve this quadrant for the Spanish moss, which needs more space to fill in evenly.

2. Fill one quadrant with polished river stones, confining them to their section by selecting larger stones to edge the rectangle. Fill the gaps with smaller stones so that the floral foam doesn't show through. Fill an adjoining quadrant with marble river gravel, keeping it within the rectangle's borders.

3. Measure one side of the third quadrant. Cut lengths of bamboo to this measurement, using a craft saw and cutting mat. Cut as many as are needed to fill the quadrant, mixing thick and thin stalks for variety, if desired.

4. Fill the remaining, deeper quadrant with Spanish moss until it reaches the same level as the stones and bamboo. Place dried strawflowers in a random pattern on the centerpiece's surface.

pea pod vase

There's nothing sweeter than peas picked fresh from the garden! But do save
one pod to imprint this air-dried, paint-glazed terra-cotta vase.

MATERIALS

pea stalk with pea pod and leaves

Mexican terra-cotta clay

waterproof sealer

craft acrylic paint in white and soft green

premixed acrylic painting glaze
in metallic gold

spray matte acrylic varnish

rolling pin*

craft knife

scissors

soft paintbrushes

foam brush

clean, soft cloth

disposable container with cover

templates (see page 297)

*Reserved for craft use

1. Photocopy the patterns (page 297) onto plain paper, and cut out them out to make the templates.

2. Place a small handful of clay in a disposable container. Cover with water, seal the container, and let sit overnight. This makes "slip," a jellylike substance that will be used later to adhere the clay slabs together.

3. On a protected work surface, roll out a slab of clay to a ¼" (5 mm) thickness. Place the template pieces on the clay surface, and cut out the shapes with a craft knife. Remove the excess clay.

4. Place a pea pod with a small amount of stem on an angle near the top of the rectangular slab. Add groups of leaves, vein side down, and tendrils, creating a pleasing pattern around the pod. Be sure to place the pod and stems at an angle to the sides of the slab, or they will crack open when the vase is assembled.

5. Roll the rolling pin over the pea leaves and pod, pressing them into the clay. Don't roll too heavily over the pod. Carefully press each leaf even more firmly into the clay with your fingers.

6. Score a row of X's along the two shorter side edges of the slab. Use a soft brush to apply slip to these edges. With the pea greens still embedded in the clay, shape the slab into a cylinder, butting the short edges. Score a ring of X's on the sides of the circular base and the bottom inside edge of the cylinder. Brush the scored edges with slip, and join the base to the cylinder. Carefully remove the pea greens. Wipe the joined edges with a soft brush and more slip until well sealed and smooth. Let dry for 48 hours.

7. Apply water-based sealer inside and out with a foam brush, and let dry. Dip a clean cloth in white acrylic paint. Working in horizontal strokes, wipe a coat of paint across the vase. Make sure that the pea and leaf impressions fill with paint to accent them. Wipe away the excess paint to leave a light wash. Let dry.

8. With a small soft brush, apply green acrylic paint to the leaves and pea pod, and again wipe away the excess to leave a soft color-washed surface. Let dry.

9. Using a clean cloth, wipe a light coat of premixed metallic gold decorative painter's glaze across the surface of the vase. Wipe away any excess paint as desired and let dry. Spray with one coat of matte finish acrylic varnish.

BRANCHING OUT

Make a few small clay pieces with pea
imprints on them for experimentation
with different finishes—try a dark brown
wash to accent the imprints, or any other
combination of acrylic paints, rub-on wax
finishes, or paint glazes. You can also
make flower or fall leaf imprints in the clay.

THE INSIDE DIRT

• You don't need a garden plot to make this
  project—the peas used to imprint this
  vase were grown in containers on a deck.

• This project can be ideal for peas that
  have passed their peak of sweetness.
  Peas with toughened pods that are more
  pronounced in form will make well-
  defined imprints.

BRANCHING OUT

Mulberry paper provides the perfect absorbent yet lightweight paper for screened projects. Watercolor paper is a good choice for flower-pounding projects that require a heavier paper. Create special greeting cards and frameable art from your pounded flower experiments. Or, fill a journal, writing the name of each flower next to the pounded print for future reference. You can also pound flowers onto fabric treated with a mordant.

THE INSIDE DIRT

• Of the many flowers tested for this project, cosmos, pansies, scavola, and rose vinca were superior. Pink impatiens created a subtle but pleasant dye transfer. Note that white flowers do not transfer, not even onto dark-colored paper.

• If a flower's pistil is fleshy, it will get mashed in the transfer and ruin the paper. In such cases, pluck the petals individually and transfer in a reassembled form.

pounded flower night-light shade

Flower pounding provides immediate gratification—the beauty of the natural dyes from freshly picked flowers is intense and evocative. This shoji screen—inspired shade can be hung on a small nail in front of a wall outlet to give a conventional night-light a new look. Leave the sides of the shade open for easy access to the night-light's on-off switch, or line the sides with more pounded leaf prints.

MATERIALS

assorted fresh flowers*

mulberry paper

¼" x ¼" (5 mm x 5 mm) basswood, four 6" (15 cm) strips

¼" x ¹⁄₁₆" (5 mm x 1 mm) basswood, two 4½" (11 cm) strips, two 4" (10 cm) strips, and four 2" (5 cm) strips

black acrylic paint

white craft glue

PVA glue (neutral pH adhesive)

hammer

foam brush

paper towel

*Recommended are cosmos, rose vinca, scavola, and pink cascading petunias

1. Place a sheet of mulberry paper on top of four sheets of paper towel. Lay your chosen freshly picked flowers facedown on the mulberry paper, and cover with an additional paper towel. Pound the surface with a hammer until you see the natural flower dyes seep through the top paper towel. You can check your progress by lifting just the edge of a petal. Make sure that you've pounded all the surface area of the flower for an even transfer to the mulberry paper. Peel off the flower, and let the transfer dry. Not all flowers will transfer well; be prepared to experiment with many varieties, and watch them over time. Some will seem to work but then fade or discolor over the course of a few days.

2. Paint the twelve basswood strips with black acrylic paint. Let dry. To assemble the front frame, use white glue to join two 4½" (11 cm) and two 6" (15 cm) strips together, allowing a ¼" (5 mm) overhang at all corners. For the back frame, glue two 4" (10 cm) and two 6" (15 cm) strips together, overhanging at the top and bottom edges only. Let dry.

3. Join the front and back frames at the longer edges by gluing on four 2" (5 cm) strips, two on each side, to make a three-dimensional box. Hold together by hand for a few minutes, or until the glue sets. Support, if necessary, and let dry completely.

4. Trim one pounded flower print into a rectangle that will fit inside the front frame. Fold the long edges of the paper rectangle to lay flat against the vertical basswood strips. Brush PVA glue on the four inside edges of the front frame. Place the paper rectangle against the glued surface, and run your finger lightly along the edges to seal the paper firmly to the basswood frame. Let dry. Glue flower print panels in the side frames if desired.

money plant and
bamboo lamp shade

Delicately shingled money plant seed pods add fragile elegance to a purchased lamp shade.
Bamboo stalks define the faces of the shade and add their unique texture to the finished project.

MATERIALS

money plant seed pods

bamboo

white four-sided lamp shade

low-temperature glue gun

glue sticks

fine-blade craft saw

scissors

1 Cut the money plant seed pods from their stalks with scissors.

2 Place the lamp shade on the lamp base to suspend it above your work surface. Work on one plane surface of the shade at a time. Using the glue gun, apply a bead of glue horizontally across the bottom edge. Quickly and firmly press money plant seed pods in a row along the glue line, overlapping them slightly and overhanging the bottom edge of the shade.

3 Apply a second horizontal bead of glue just above the first row of seed pods. Place a second row of seed pods, over-lapping the first row in a shingle pattern. Continue gluing on seed pods in rows until one face of the shade is covered. Repeat for the remaining sides.

4 Using a fine-blade craft saw, cut four lengths of bamboo to conceal each corner edge of the shade. Glue in place. In the same way, cut four shorter lengths to trim the top edges, and glue in place.

BRANCHING OUT

You can cover a cone-shaped lamp shade, too—just skip the top edging of bamboo and extend the side bamboo accents past the top and bottom of the shade to mimic an umbrella frame. The delicate money plant "shingles" are not appropriate for projects that will receive a lot of handling. Save them for decorative vases, night-lights, wall sconces, and paneled screens.

THE INSIDE DIRT

- Money plant, also known as honesty, is a natural for air-drying. Just hang it by the stem.

- You can also use silica gel to dry the money plant's seed pods.

The following pages contain an array of simple ideas and quick ways to bring the garden into your home. Each includes brief crafting tips, how-to instructions, and/or variation suggestions. And each is meant to underscore how

gallery of quick decorating ideas

garden-grown items and found objects can be used to make simple, low-budget gifts and decorative accents. Let the ideas you find here trigger brainstorms of your own. Like any true gardener or crafter, you are always ready to be inspired. Be resourceful, expect the unexpected, and enjoy the process.

chili pepper kitchen accents

Here's a hot tip: Add spice to your kitchen decor with dried chili peppers! String them on lightweight wire along with painted glass beads and dried peli nuts (both easily found in bead stores) to make a stylish window swag. Or, hot-glue a few peppers to the top of a wooden recipe box. For a rustic finish, color the box with water-based cranberry stain, sand the edges, and top with a light wash of white pickling gel. Drying peppers is as easy as drying flowers. Harvest them when ripe, then string them in bunches through their stems using a needle and thread. Hang them in a well-ventilated location until they are dry. Note: Use caution when handling chili peppers to avoid skin and eye irritaion.

sunflower curtain tieback

This curtain is cinched with a ribbon made from thinly peeled bark and studded with a single bright, wispy sunflower. The large flower was dried in two stages. First, it was set facedown in silica gel. Once the petals were dry, it was turned over and and the thick calyx and stem were sunk into the gel. To prevent the delicate petals from breaking off, a clear-drying glue was applied to the base of each one. The flower stem was inserted through a small hole in the ribbon and glued in place.

garden spigot hooks

Here's a whimsical way to hang your garden tools and sun hat. Create a series of hooks with purchased or vintage garden spigots and wooden rosettes—unfinished ornamental squares with a circular design already cut onto the surface. First, finish the wood rosettes as desired. We chose bright oil-based stains that are heavily pigmented yet transparent (see Craft Resources on page 298). Then, mount a spigot to the center of each rosette with two brass screws. Look for spigots with a notched flange for easy assembly.

burlap floor cloth with vegetable-dyed trim

Dyeing is a subtle but time-honored way to make botanicals a component of your handcrafted projects. Here, a burlap floor cloth is trimmed with a beet-dyed fringe. Some garden plants are classics for making natural dyes: yarrow, goldenrod, marigold, blueberries, tomatoes (the skins only), beets, and cranberries. But nearly every plant will yield some color, whether it's from the leaves, fruit, petals, bark, or roots. Often, a mordant is used with natural dyes to help set the color. The most common and least toxic mordant is aluminum potassium sulfate, also known as alum or alum salt. Used sometimes in pickling, alum may be purchased in most grocery stores.

garden boutonniere

Half the fun of growing your own fruits and vegetables is preserving the bounty in the form of jams, chutneys, sauces, and relishes to enjoy and share throughout the year. Instead of sticking the same predictable label on your canning jars, use natural resources from your garden to decorate the packaging. Here, elements from a berry plant were used as an identifying "boutonniere" for a jar of strawberry jam. What looks like a flower on this simple boutonniere is actually the leafy top of a strawberry. The top was hollowed out and dried in silica gel. An immature berry, plucked from the strawberry plant once it stopped bearing fruit, was dried and inserted through the top's hollow center. For a jar of pickles, you could use a dill blossom. But don't feel obligated to coordinate the boutonniere to the jar's contents. A dried flower would look just as attractive.

pressed petal
votive candles

If you have just a few pressed blooms left over from a project,

try this quick technique for decorating purchased votive candles.

Simply brush the side of a candle with candle and soap medium,

a fast-drying liquid that seals wax finishes. While the medium

is still wet, press the botanicals onto the candle surface. Brush

a second coat of the medium over the flowers to seal them in place,

and let dry. Clever arrangements of clover leaves, phlox, primroses,

bidens, and hydrangea petals can add pattern and color to plain

candles. Do a test candle with each botanical first, as some flowers

lose their pigmentation after exposure to the candle medium. And,

as always, carefully monitor votive candles while they are lit.

kitchen herb bouquet vase

When your garden is bursting with fresh herbs, bring daily clippings into the kitchen so they are readily at hand as you cook. For a simple, poetic touch, place them in cylindrical vases, shown here wrapped in a rice paper with springlike, spearmint-colored striping. The paper is lashed in place with hemp twine, making it easy to change papers with the seasons or on a whim. For an accent, insert a twig from a wild grapevine through each knot. You might also try a dried flower.

espresso cup centerpiece

Brighten up your table setting with tiny espresso cups filled with mini bouquets of dried flowers or dried petals, such as our bunches of two air-dried strawflower varieties, desiccant-dried species rose petals, and screen-dried species roses. When the party's over, let guests take their cups home as favors. If you're feeling extra creative, put a "green thumb" on each purchased cup using a thumbprint stamp and green oven-firing craft enamel paint made especially for use on already glazed ceramics. Simply paint the stamp's printing surface with the enamel, blot lightly on a paper towel, and press onto the surface of the cup, carefully rolling the stamp once from side to side for even coverage. Mistakes can easily be wiped from the cups with a damp cloth before baking. Follow the paint manufacturer's directions for surface preparation and oven firing. Tip: If your bouquets need a bit more stability to stand straight, fill the cup partway with dried beans to provide a base for the stems.

layered petal centerpiece

Make a room bloom with unexpected color as well as graphic style when you layer petals in a decon-structed potpourri. Combine different shapes of clear glassware as we have here, and fill them with complementary colors for a group centerpiece. Or, fill a single large glass vase or canning jar with layer upon layer of petals. We've combined lavender with Iona (African daisies), red garden rose petals with statice, and pink cluster roses, heads still intact, with their leaves. All of the flowers were air-dried.

dahlia and moss picture frame

Revitalize a flea market find with dried flowers, sheet moss, and a glue gun. First, paint an unfin-

ished or unattractive frame with a coat of olive green acrylic paint, and let dry. Apply sheet moss

to the frame's surface with a low-temperature glue gun. Finally, glue desiccant-dried yellow dahlias

randomly on the surface. Your final product will make a sunny, carefree addition to your home.

Try other combinations of dried botanicals, too, with or without the moss underlayer.

flower art

Use antique wallpaper to create romantic, vintage settings for your favorite blooms. If you don't have sheets of old wallpaper, improvise with color photocopies of new vinyl wall coverings (paint and wall-paper stores often have sample books of discontinued wallpapers that they will give you for free) or sheets of paper gift wrap. Cut a piece of basswood to the size of the frame backing, and glue the wallpaper (or facsimile) to it using acrylic matte medium or wallpaper paste. When the glue is dry, sand the paper lightly to distress the finish, and age it by applying an uneven wash of strong cold tea. When the piece is completely dry, attach your chosen botanicals to the paper surface with a low-temperature glue gun or tacky floral glue. Desiccant-dried dahlia and air-dried cornflowers and bleeding heart are shown here.

french country hanging pots

Add Mediterranean flair to your patio or entryway by stringing together small terra-cotta pots that have been colorwashed in a bright French country palette. Begin by painting the pots with yellow and blue acrylic paint, brushing smoothly in one direction and then wiping off some of the wet color with a paper towel to reveal streaks of the underlying terra-cotta. Next, run string or twine through the drainage hole of each pot, knotting it at the point where each pot will sit. Tie a loop at the top for hanging, fill the pots with bunches of dried flowers, and voilà! Shown here are air-dried asters and statice and desiccant-dried marigold heads.

templates
and diagrams

Several of the projects in this book require templates or diagrams. To make a template, trace or photocopy the pattern printed in this section and then cut it out, as directed in the project instructions. Use the diagrams to guide you in cutting and placement decisions as you make a project.

Photocopy at 100%

12

3

6

9

sage-lined bolster (shown on pages 240–241)

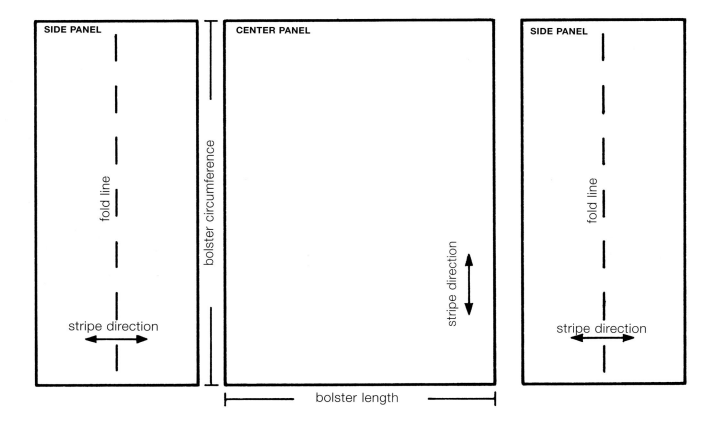

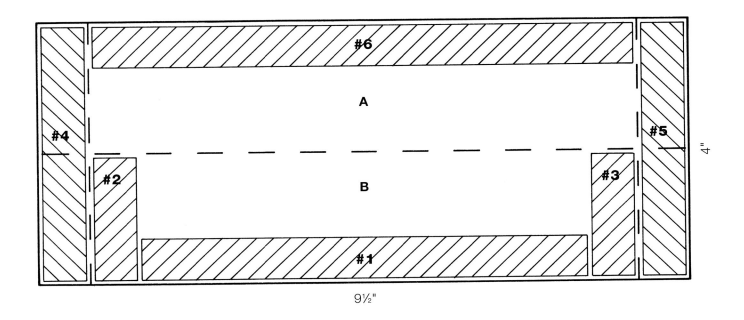

#6

A

#4

#5

#2

B

#3

#1

4"

9½"

///// ⅝" (2 cm) paper-backed fusing tape

flower waters in etched bottles

(shown on pages 248–249)

Photocopy at 100%

pea pod vase (shown on pages 258–259)

Photocopy at 100%

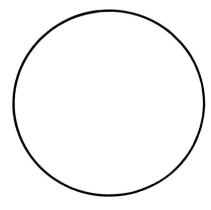

Adirondack Designs
350 Cypress Street
Fort Bragg, CA 95437
800-222-0343
www.adirondackdesign.com

Anna French Ltd.
343 Kinds Road
London SW3 5GS
United Kingdom
0207-351-1126
To the Trade Only
(fabric)

Annieglass
310 Harvest Drive
Watsonville, CA 95076
800-347-6133
(glass accessories)

Anthropologie
235 S 17th Street
Philadelphia, PA 19103
215-564-2313
www.anthropologie.com

Aptare
691 Saint Ann's Drive
Laguna Beach CA 92651
714-497-6279
(teak furniture)

Archiped Classics
315 Cole Street
Dallas, TX 75207
214-748-7437
(cast stone accessories)

Aria
295-6 Upper Street
London N1 2TU
United Kingdom
0207-704-1999
(contemporary furniture and
accessories)

Archie's Island Furniture
48 Everett Avenue
Winchester, MA 01890
800-486-1183
www.outdoormodern.com

Atlantic Yard
2424 East Las Olas Boulevard
Fort Lauderdale, FL
877-552-3516
www.atlanticyard.com
(garden products)

Avant Garden
The Studio
3 Dartmouth Place
London W4 2RH
United Kingdom
020-08747-1794

Barlow Tyrie
1263 Glen Avenue, Suite 230
Moorestown, NJ 08057
609-273-7878
(teak furniture)

Barnwood Originals
Box 906
Cochrane, Alberta
Canada, TOL 0W0
403-932-2470
(historic wood furniture)

Brown Jordon Co.
9860 Gidley Street
El Monte, CA 91731
626-443-8971
www.brownjordancompany.com
(metal furniture)

Capital Garden Products
Schieren Associates, Ltd.
P.O. Box 400
Pottervielle, NJ 07979
800-524-1270

Carruth Studio
1178 Farnsworth Road
Waterville, OH 43566
www.carruthstudio.com
(cast-concrete and terra-cotta stat-
ues)

Casual Comforts
10025 Southeast Cindy Lane
Boring, OR 97009
503-663-6401

Catalonia Collections
1503 Caheuenga Boulevard
Los Angeles, CA 90028
213-469-5266

Charleston Gardens
P.O. Box 20730
Charleston, SC 29413
800-469-0118
www.charlestongardens.com

Chelsea Ex-Centrics
297 Kansas Street, Suite B
San Francisco, CA 94103
415-863-4868

Classic Garden Ornaments
Longshadow Gardens
83 Longshadow Lane
Pomona, IL 62975

Colonial Williamsburg
P.O. Box 3532
Williamsburg, VA 23185
800-446-9240
www.williamsburgmarketplace.com
(accessories)

Country Casual
17317 Germantown Road
Germantown, MD 20874
301-540-0040
www.countrycasual.com
(high-quality teak furniture)

Crate & Barrel
311 Gilman Avenue
P.O. Box 9059
Wheeling, IL 60090
800-451-8217
www.crateandbarrel.com

Ilan Dei
1227 Abbot Kinney Boulevard
Venice, CA 90291
310-450-0999

Dominic Capon
Unit 9, Imperial Studios
Imperial Road
London SW6 2AG
United Kingdom
0207-736-3060
(accessories from India & Vietnam)

Durasol Systems, Inc.
197 Stone Castle Road
Rock Tavern, NY 12575
914-778-1000
888-822-0383
www.durasol.com
(retractable awnings)

Jacqueline Edge
1 Courtnell Street
London W2 5BU
United Kingdom
0207-229-1172
(ornaments, loungers, bamboo
deckchairs)

The Elegant Earth
1301 First Avenue North
Birmingham, AL 35203
800-242-7758

Elizabeth Street Gardens & Gallery
1176 Second Avenue
New York, NY 10021
(nineteenth-century French cast-
iron sculptures, decorative urns,
etc.)

Ethan Allen
Ethan Allen Drive
PO Box 1966
Danbury, CT 06813
800-228-9229
www.ethanallen.com
(furniture)

Florentine Craftsmen Inc.
46-24 28th Street
Long Island City, NY 11101
(lead and cast-iron furniture and
ornaments)

The Flower Depot
P.O. Box 654
Tonganoxie, KS 66086
1-877-780-2099
www.flowerdepotstore.com
www.thewreathdepot.com
(dried and preserved botanicals, wreaths, swags, and craft
supplies)

French Wyres
P.O. Box 131655
Tyler, TX 75713
903-561-1752
www.frenchwyres.com
(wire furniture and plant
stands)

Frontier Barnwood
3205 Erie Street
Laramie, WY 82070
307-742-5248
(weathered wood accessories)

Garden Concepts Collection
P.O. Box 241233
Memphis, TN 38124
901-756-1649
www.gardenconcepts.net

Gardener's Eden
1655 Bassford Drive
Mexico, MO 65265
800-822-9600

Gardener's Supply Co.
128 Intervale Road
Burlington, VT 05401
800-836-1700
www.gardeners.com

Gaze Burvill
Newtonwood Workshop
Newton Valence
Alton, Hampshire GU34 3 EW
England
United Kingdom
0142-058-7467
www.gazeburvill.com
(high-quality contemporary
furniture)

Giati Designs, Inc.
614 Santa Barbara Street
Santa Barbara, CA 93101
805-965-6535

The Glidden Company
925 Euclid Avenue
Cleveland, OH 44115
800-221-4100
www.gliddenpaints.com

Gloss Ltd
274 Portobello Road
London W10 5TE
United Kingdom
0208-960-4146
e-mail: pascale@glassltd
   .u-net.com
(soft furnishings)

Haddonstone (USA) Ltd.
5362 Industrial Drive
Huntington Beach, CA 92649
714-894-3500
(cast reconstituted limestone
accessories)

Home Depot
www.HomeDepot.com

IKEA
1100 Broadway Mall
Hicksville, NY 11801
519-681-4532
www.ikea.com
(Scandinavian-style furniture)

Barbara Israel Garden Antiques
296 Mount Holly Road
Katonah, NY 10536
212-744-6281
www.bi-gardenantiques.com
(period American and European
antiques)

John Kelly Furniture Design
144 Cambers Street
New York, NY 10007
212-385-1885

Cath Kidston
8 Clarendon Cross
London W11 4AP
United Kingdom
0207-221-4000
www.cathkidston.co.uk
(vintage & floral fabrics, furniture,
and accessories)

Kingsley-Bate
5587B Guinea Road
Fairfax, VA 22032
703-978-7200
www.kingsleybate.com
(high-quality teak furniture)

Kinsman Company, Inc.
River Road
Point Pleasant, PA 18950
800-733-4146
(terra cotta accessories)

Knoll, Inc.
1235 Water Street
East Greenville, PA 18041
800-445-5045

Lister Lutyens
Hammonds Drive
Eastbourne, East Sussex BN23
6PW
England
United Kingdom
0132-343-1177
www.lister-lutyens.co.uk
(high-quality teak furniture)

Llyod/Flanders Industries
3010 Tenth Street
Menominee, MI 49858
800-526-9894
(all-weather wicker furniture)

Loose Ends LLC
P.O. Box 20310
Keizer, OR 97307
503-390-2348
503-390-4724 (fax)
www.looseends.com
(papers, dried botanicals, home
and garden accessories)

Kennetth Lynch & Sons
84 Danbury Road
Wilton, CT 06897
203-762-8363
www.lkynchsons.com
(garden ornaments)

Malabar
31-3 South Bank Business Centre
London SW8 5BL
United Kingdom
0207-501-4220
(Indian silks and natural cottons)

Maine Cottage Furniture
P.O. Box 935
Yarmouth, ME 04096
207-846-1430

Maine Millstones/Royal
Stonework
Southport, Maine 04576
207-633-6091
(fountains)

Majestic
80 Cherry Street
Bridgeport, CT 06605
203-367-7900
(accessories)

McGuire
1201 Bryant Street
San Francisco, CA 94103
415-626-1414

McKinnon & Harris, Inc.
P.O. Box 4885
Richmond, VA23220
804-358-2385

Meyers Imports
215 Frobisher Drive
Waterloo, ON, N2VV 2G4
Canada
800-267-8562
(importer of European garden
products)

Minh Mong
182 Battersea Park Road
London SW11 2RW
United Kingdom
0207-498-3233
e-mail: minhmong@lineone.net
(Vietnamese and Cambodian
silks)

The Modern Garden Co.
Hill Pasture, Brosted, Great
Dunmow
Essex CM6 2BZ
London
United Kingdom
www.moderngarden.co.uk
(modern garden furniture in
plastic, steel, aluminum, con-
crete, and contemporary fabrics)

Mottahedeh
225 Fifth Avenue
New York, NY 10010
212-685-3050

Natural Decorations, Inc. (NDI)
777 Industrial Park Drive
Brewton, AL 36426
800-522-2627
www.ndi.com

Old Hickory Furniture Co., Inc.
403 South Noble Street
Shelbyville, IN 46176
800-232-2275

Pier 1 Imports
800-245-4595
www.pier1.com

Pottery Barn
P.O. Box 379905
Las Vegas, NV 89137
800-588-6250
www.potterybarn.com

Reed Bros.
Turner Station
Sebastopol, CA 95472
707-795-6261

Richardson Allen
P.O. Box 236
Saco, ME 04072
207-284-8402

Dez Ryan Studio
156 Chambers Street
Third floor
New York, NY 10007
212-693-0263
(glass accessories)

Richard Schultz
806 Gravel Pike
P.O. Box 96
Palm, PA 18070
215-679-2222
(furniture)

Seibert & Rice
P.O. Box 365
Short Hills, NJ 07078
973-367-8266
www.seibert-rice.com
(terra-cotta pots)

Smith & Hawkin
P.O. Box 431
Milwaukee, WI 53201
800-776-3336
www.smithandhawken.com

Stone Forest
Department F
P.O. Box 2840
Santa Fe, NM 87504
505-986-8883
(hand-carved granite, Japanese
traditional design)

Summit Furniture, Inc.
5 Harris Court
Monterey, CA 93940
408-375-7811

Terra Furniture, Inc.
17855 Arenth Avenue
City of Industry, CA 91748
818-912-8523

Tropitone Furniture
5 Marconi
Irvine, CA 92618
714-951-2010

The Veneman Collection
6392 Industry Way
Westminster, CA 92683
714-894-0202

Vermont Outdoor Furniture
Barre, VT
800-588-8834
www.vermontoutdoorfurniture.
com
(northern white cedar furniture)

Weatherend Estate Furniture
6 Gordon Drive
Rockland, ME 04841
207-596-6483

Whisper Glide Swing Company
22233 Keather Avenue North
Forrest Lake, MN 55025

The Wicker Works
267 Eight Street
San Francisco, CA 94103
415-626-6730
(high-quality teak and wicker)

Wickets Garden Style
P.O. Box 1225
Middleburg, VA 20118
800-585-1225

Windsor Designs
475 Grant Avenue
Phoenixville, PA 19460
610-935-7777

craft resources

Britex Fabrics
146 Geary Street
San Francisco, CA 94108
415-392-2910
www.britexfabrics.com
info@britexfabrics.com
(four floors' worth of fabric, buttons, ribbons, trim, and notions;
fabric swatches available by mail
for a small fee)

Delta Ceramcoat
Whittier, CA 90601
www.deltacrafts.com
(candle and soap painting medium,
acrylic paints, and sealers)

From Nature With Love
890 Garrison Avenue
Bronx, NY 10474
1-888-376-6695
www.fromnaturewithlove.com
(melt-and-pour soap bases, wide
selection of essential oils, soap
molds, and other soap-making
supplies)

Gane Brothers & Lane, Inc.
1-800-323-0586
(distributors of Yes! Glue, a thick,
transparent paste-glue with very
good lay-flat properties for paper)

HobbyCraft
(stores nationwide)
Head Office
Bournemouth
United Kingdom
0120-259-6100
(basic craft supplies)

John Lewis
(stores nationwide)
Head Office
Oxford Street
London W1A 1EX
United Kingdom
0207-269-7711
(basic craft supplies)

Michaels
1-800-642-4235
michaels.com
(silica gel desiccant, wide selection
of craft supplies)

Mosaic Mercantile
P.O. Box 78206
San Francisco, CA 94107
877-9-MOSAIC
415-282-5413 (fax)
877-708-2111 (toll-free fax)
www.mosaicmercantile.com
(mosaic tile, grouts, primers, and
adhesives)

Nature's Pressed
P.O. Box 212
Orem, UT 84059
801-225-1169
800-850-2499
801-225-1760 (fax)
www.naturespressed.com
(flower presses; pressed flowers,
ferns, foliage, herbs, and leaves)

Pebeo of America, Inc.
P.O. Box 717
555 Route 78, Airport Road
Swanton, VT 05488
819-829-5012
819-821-4151 (fax)
www.pebeo.com
(Setacolor Soleil Sunprinting
Paint, 20 water-based, brilliant
colors; completely nontoxic, mix-
able, and permanent once
ironed)

Rubber Stamps of America
160 Emerald St
Keene, NH 03431
800-553-5031
603-352-0265 (fax)
www.stampusa.com
(rubber thumbprint stamp)

Walnut Hollow
1409 State Road 23
Dodgeville, WI 53533-2112
800-950-5101
(unfinished wood crafts available
at leading craft departments
throughout the country; call for
the nearest location)

Woodburst Color Company
www.woodburst.com
(brightly colored transparent pigmented oil-based stain)

Lighting

The Lighting Edge/Altec Lighting
50 West Avenue
P.O. Box 925
Essex, CT 06426
860-787-8968
www.lightingedge.com

Architectural Area Lighting
14249 Artesian Boulevard
La Mirada, CA 90638
704-994-2700
www.aal.net

Dover Design Inc.
2175 Beaver Valley Pike
New Providence, PA 17560
(handcrafted copper landscape
lights)

Escort Lighting
51 North Elm Street
Wernersville, PA 19565
800-856-7948

Hanover Lanterns Terralight
470 High Street
Hanover, PA 17331

Liteform Designs
P.O. Box 3316
Portland, OR 97208

Stonelight Corp.
2701 Gulf Shore Boulevard North
Naples, FL 33940

Paving, Walling, Timber, and Stone

Anchor Block Co.
2300 McKnight Road
North St. Paul, MN 55109
651-777-8321
www.anchorblock.com

Ann Sacks Tile and Stone
115 Steward Street
Seattle WA 98101
www.annsacks.com

Bamboo Fencer
179 Boylston Street
Jamaica Plain, MA 02130
617-524-6137
www.bamboofencer.com

Classical Flagstones
Lower Ledge Farm
Doynton Lane
Dyrham, Wilshire SN14 8EY
United Kingdom
www.classical-flagstones.com

Cold Spring Granite Company
202 South Third Avenue
Cold Spring, MN 56320
www.coldspringgranite.com

Eco Timber International
P.O. Box 882461
San Francisco, CA 94188
888-801-0855
www.ecotimber.com

Fiberstars, Inc.
2883 Bayview Drive
Fremont, CA 94538
510-490-0719
(fiber optic FiberScape paver system)

Goshen Stone
P.O. Box 332
Goshen, MA 01032
413-268-7171
www.goshenstone.co
(micaschist flagstone)

Halquist Stone
P.O. Box 308
Sussex, WI 53089
800-255-8811
www.limestone.com

Imagine Tile
10 Exchange Place
Suite 2010
Jersey City, NJ 07302
800-680-8453
(graphic ceramic floor tiles)

Pine Hall Brick Company
P.O. Box 11011
Winston Salem, NC 27116
800-334-8689
www.pinehallbrick.com
(specialty bricks)

Annie Sabroux Studio
2001 Main Street
Santa Monica, CA 90405
310-399-7037
(site-specific mosaics)

Syndecrete
2908 Colorado Avenue
Santa Monica, CA 90404
310-829-9932
(lightweight concrete)

The Timber Source
P.O. Box 100
Winchester, KY 40392
859-744-9700
(info on North American woods
from sustainable forests)

Wausau Tile Inc.
P.O. Box 1520
Wausau, WI 54401
800-388-8738
www.traditional-building.com

Structures

Amdega Ltd.
Faverdale, Darington Co.
Durham, England DL3 0PW
United Kingdom
080-059-1523
Design offices through the US
and Canada, 800-449-7348
Ireland, Europe, and Asia, 44-
132-546-8522
info@amedga.co.uk
www.amdega.com
(conservatories and other garden
structures)

The Bank
1824 Felicity Street
New Orleans, LA 70113
(architectural elements)

Bow House Inc.
92 Randall Road
Boston, MA 01740
978-779-6464

Dalton Pavilions Inc.
20 Commerce Drive
Telford, PA 18969-1030
215-721-1492
www.daltonpavilions.com

Four Seasons Solar Products
5005 Veterans Memorial Highway
Holbrook, NY 11741-4516
806-368-7732
www.four-seasons-
sunrooms.com

Trellis Structures
P.O. Box 380
Beverly, MA 01915
978-921-1235
www.trellisstructures.com

Vixen Hill Gazebos
Main Street
Elverston, PA 19520
800-423-2766
www.vixenhill.com

design resources

Joe Addo
Joe Addo Studio
9312 Civic Center Drive
Beverly Hills, CA 90210
310-274-4333

Michael and Hilary Anderson
Clacton & Frinton
107 South Robertson Boulevard
Los Angeles, CA 90048
310-275-1967

Hideaki Ariizumi
Gynis M. Berry
Studio A/B
111 Fourth Avenue
Number 2M
New York, NY 10003
212-677-7898

David E. Austin, AIA
Dana Marcu
Austin Patterson Associates
Architects
376 Pequot Avenue
P.O. Box 61
Southport, CT 06490
203-255-4031

Barbara Barry
Barbara Barry Incorporated
9526 Pico Boulevard
Los Angeles, CA 90035
310-275-9977

Hagy Belzberg
Belzberg Architects
9615 Brighton Way
Suite 320
Beverly Hills, CA 90210
310-271-3087

James Blakeley, III, ASID
Blakeley-Bazeley, Ltd.
P.O.Box 5173
Beverly Hills, CA 90210
213-653-3548

Peter Q. Bohlin, FAIA
Bernard J. Cywinski, FAIA
Jon C. Jackson, AIA
Bohlin Cywinski Jackson
125 South Ninth Street
Philadelphia, PA 19107
215-592-0600

Stanley Boles
Kevin Johnson
John O'Toole
BOORA Architects, Inc.
720 Southwest Washington
Portland, OR 97205
503-226-1575

Pamela Burton
Burton & Company Landscape
Architecture
2324 Michigan Avenue
Santa Monica, CA 90404
310-828-6373

Aviva Bornovski Carmy
Holly Bieniewski, AIA
Carmy Design Group
10793 Lindbrook Drive
Los Angeles, CA 90024
310-446-9556

Victoria Casasco
Victoria Casasco Studio
320D Sunset Avenue
Venice, CA 90291
310-399-1206

Richard Corsini
Richard Corsini Architect
2841 Avenel Street
Los Angeles, CA 90039
213-662-0752

Ilan Dei
1227 Abbot Kinney Boulevard
Venice, CA 90291
310-450-0999

Mayita Dinos
310-838-5959

Tony Duquette
1354 Dawnridge Drive
Beverly Hills, CA 90202
310-271-3574

Steven Ehrlich, FAIA
Steven Ehrlich Architects
2210 Colorado Avenue
Santa Monica, CA 90404
310-828-6700

John Erickson, AIA
Erickson Designs
24443 Zermatt Lane
Valencia, CA 91355

James Estes
James Estes and Company
Architects
79 Thames Street
Newport, RI 02840
401-846-3336

Bernardo Fort-Brescia, FAIA
Laurinda Hope Spear, FAIA
Arquitectonica
550 Brickell Avenue
Suite 200
Miami, FL 33131
305-372-1812

Susan Jay Freeman, ASID
Susan Jay Design
9009 Beverly Boulevard
Los Angeles, CA 90048
310-858-1181

Ron Goldman, FAIA
Bob Firth, AIA
Clelio Boccato, AIA
Goldman Firth Boccato
Architects
24955 Pacific Coast Highway
Suite A202
Malibu, CA 90265
310-456-1831

Alexander Gorlin
Alexander Gorlin Architect
137 Varick Street
New York, NY 10013
212-229-1199

David Lawrence Gray, FAIA
David Lawrence Gray Architects,
AIA
1546 Seventh Street
Suite 101
Santa Monica, CA 90401
310-394-5707

David Hacin
Hacin & Associates Architects
46 Waltham Street
Suite 404
Boston, MA 02118
617-426-0077

David Hertz, AIA
Syndesis
2908 Colorado Avenue
Santa Monica, CA 90404
310-829-9932

Charlie Hess
C. Hess Design
516 North Mansfield
Los Angeles, CA 90036
213-930-1706

Aleks Istanbullu
Aleks Istanbullu John Kaliski
Architecture and City Design
1659 Eleventh Street
Suite 200
Santa Monica, CA 90404
310-450-8246

Albert Janz, IIDA
Sherry Stein
Henry Johnstone & Company
95 San Miguel Road
Pasadena, CA 91105
626-395-9528

Noel Jeffrey
Noel Jeffrey Inc. Interior Design
215 East 58th Street
New York, NY 10022
212-935-7775

Sarah Boyer Jenkins, FASID
Edward Wesely
Sarah Boyer Jenkins and
Associates, Inc.
8520 Connecticut Avenue
Suite 101
Chevy Chase, MD 20815
301-951-3880

Debbie Jones
310-476-1824

Chip Kalleen, IIDA
Old Hickory Furniture Co., Inc.
403 South Noble Street
Shelbyville, IN 46176
800-232-2275

Annie Kelly
2074 Watsonia Terrace
Hollywood, CA 90068
213-874-4278

Christine Kendall-Jent, ASID,
IIDA
Santa Barbara Interiors
450 Paseo Del Descanso
Santa Barbara, CA 93105
805-569-1937

Mark D. Kirkhart, AIA
William S. Wolf
DesignARC, Inc.
One North Salsipuedes Street
Suite 210
Santa Barbara, CA 93105
805-963-4401

Sandy Koepke
Sandy Koepke Interior Design
1517 North Beverly Drive
Beverly Hills, CA 90210
310-273-1960

James Kwan
Kwan Design
409 North Lucerne Boulevard
Los Angeles, CA 90004
213-464-1032

David Lake
Ted Flato
Lake & Flato Inc.
311 Third Street
Suite 200
San Antonio, TX 78205
210-227-3335

Bill Lane
Bill Lane & Associates, Inc.
926 North Orlando Avenue
Los Angeles, CA 90069
310-657-7890

Ricardo Legorreta
Legorreta Arquitectos
Sierra Nevada No. 460
Lomas de Chapultepec, Mexico,
DF
525-520-0745

Donn Logan
ELS/Elbasani & Logan Architects
2030 Addison Street
Berkeley, CA 94704
510-549-2929

Janet Lohman
Janet Lohman Interior Design
1021 South Fairfax
Los Angeles, CA 90019
213-933-3359

Mark Mack
Mack Architects
2343 Eastern Court
Venice, CA 90291
310-822-0094

Lisa Claiborne Matthews, AIA,
ASID
1510 Abbot Kinney Boulevard
Venice, CA 90291
310-399-7108

Roy McMakin
1422 34th Avenue
Seattle, WA 98122
206-323-0198

Lee F. Mindel, AIA
Shelton, Mindel & Associates
216 West 18th Street
New York, NY 10011
212-243-3939

Brian Alfred Murphy
Julie Hart
BAM Construction/Design Inc.
150 West Channel Road
Santa Monica, CA 90402
310-459-0955

Susan Narduli, AIA
Narduli/Grinstein Architects
2304 Zeno Place
Venice, CA 90291
310-827-9697

David R. Olson, AIA
David R. Olson Architects
6 Morgan
Suite 100
Irvine, CA 92618
714-587-3041

John O'Neill
James Palmer
John O'Neill Architectural Design
508 Mystic Way
Laguna Beach, CA 92651
714-497-6170

Gary Orr
Orr Design Office
2600 San Jose Way
Sacramento, CA 95817
916-452-3642

Polly Osborne, AIA
Osborne Architects
1833 Stanford Street
Santa Monica, CA 90404
310-828-2212

McKee Patterson, AIA
Austin Patterson Associates
Architects
376 Pequot Avenue
P.O. Box 61
Southport, CT 06490
203-255-4031

Michael Palladino
Richard Meier + Partners
Architects
1001 Gayley Avenue
Los Angeles, CA 90024
310-208-6464

Rob Pressman, ASLA
TGP, Inc.
6345 Balboa Boulevard
Suite 125
Encin, CA 91316
818-345-3602

Gwynne Pugh
Larry Scarpa
Pugh + Scarpa Architecture and
Engineering
Bergamot Station
2525 Michigan Avenue
Building F1
Santa Monica, CA 90404
310-828-0226

Joseph Ruggiero
Joseph Ruggiero & Associates
4512 Louise Avenue
Encino, CA 91316
818-783-9257

Daniel Sachs
Snook
10 Greene Street
New York, NY 10013
212-343-2420

Martha Schwartz
Martha Schwartz, Inc.
147 Sherman Street
Suite 200
Cambridge, MA 02140
617-661-8141

Josh Schweitzer
Schweitzer BIM Inc.
5541 West Washington Boulevard
Los Angeles, CA 90016
213-936-6163

Russell Shubin, AIA
Robin Donaldson, AIA
Shubin + Donaldson Architects
629 State Street
Suite 242
Santa Barbara, CA 93101
805-966-2802

Kathleen Spiegelman
K. Spiegelman Interiors
623 North Almont
West Hollywood, CA 90069
310-273-2255

John Staff, AIA
J. Staff Architect
2148-C Federal Avenue
Los Angeles, CA 90025
310-477-9972

Odom and Kate Stamps
Stamps & Stamps
318 Fairview Avenue
South Pasadena, CA 91030
818-441-5600

Timothy Morgan Steele
805-965-3888

Rob Steiner
Griffith & Steiner
717 California Avenue
Venice, CA 90291
310-450-0125

Stephen Suzman
Suzman Design Associates
233 Douglass Street
San Francisco, CA 94114
415-252-0111

Brian Tichenor
Raun Thorp
Tichenor & Thorp Architects
8730 Wilshire Boulevard
Penthouse
Los Angeles, CA 90211
310-358-8444

Jeffrey Michael Tohl, AIA
The Architecture Studio
8522 West Third Street
Los Angeles, CA 90048
310-652-7890

Sallie Trout
Trout Studios
5880 Blackwelder
Culver City, CA 90232
310-202-8868

Anne Troutman
Troutman & Associates
1721 Pier Avenue
Santa Monica, CA 90405
310-452-0410

William Turnbull, Jr.
Eric Haesloop
Turnbull Griffin & Haesloop
Architects
Pier 1fi, The Embarcadero
San Francisco, CA 94111
415-986-3642

Raquel Vert
Raquel Vert Design
18039 Karen Drive
Encino, CA 91316
818-708-1177

Diego Villaseñor
Diego Villaseñor Arquitecto y
Asociados
Tiburero Montiel 96
San Miquel
Chapultepec D.F.
11850, Mexico
52-5-272-98-44

Shepard Vineburg
Shepard Vineburg Design
232 Fifth Place
Manhattan Beach, CA 90266
310-318-6810

Mark Warwick
Kim Hoffman
The System Design
9828 Charleville Boulevard
Beverly Hills, CA 90212
310-556-7711

Vicente Wolf
Vicente Wolf Associates, Inc.
333 West 39th Street
New York, NY 10018
212-465-0590

Marcy Li Wong, AIA
Marcy Li Wong Architect
2251 Fifth Street
Berkeley, CA 94710
510-843-0916

photography credits

Ed Addeo, 150
Courtesy of Amdega, Ltd., 27
Amedeo, 167 (bottom right); 175 (bottom left)
Michael Arden, 110 (top); 156
Farshid Assassi, 84
Karl A. Backus, 153
Gordon Beall, 98 (bottom); 109
Laurie Black, 88
Tom Bonner, 72; 87 (bottom); 91 (bottom); 118; 142; 175 (bottom right)
Steven Brooke, 46; 53; 81 (top)
Bobbie Bush, 183-297
Victoria Casasco, 41
Courtesy of Charleston Gardens, 79 (bottom); 181
Chuck Choi, 127
Courtesy of Classical Flagstones, 22
Dan Cornish, 83
Christopher Covey, 42; 48; 58 (top); 75; 89; 105; 130 (bottom)
Grey Crawford, 76 (bottom); 85 (top); 90; 143; 145
Charley Daniels, 27; 49
Guillaume de Laubier, 14; 16; 79 (top); 155
Carlos Domenech, 117
Carlos Domenech/Kemble Interiors, 10; 17
Carlos Domenech/John Telleria Design, 147
Mimi Drop, 67
John Reed Forsman, 125
Dan Francis, 128
Sally Gall, 134-135
Fred George, 32
Ron Goldman, 92
Alexander Gorlin, 28
Jay Graham, 111-113; 115; 121
Michael Grecco, 64
Steven A. Gunther, 108
Ron Haisfield/Courtesy of Mahan Rykiel Associates Inc., 12 (bottom)
Mick Hales, 151
Jerry Harpur, 120 (bottom); 140
Tim Harvey, 136-137
David Hertz, AIA, 44; 93 (top)
Douglas Hill, 29; 77; 93 (bottom)
Patrick House, 126
Warren Jagger, 56 (top)
Lourdes Jansana, 85 (bottom)
Len Jenshel, 31
David Lake, 39 (bottom)
Lourdes Legorreta, 70; 124
David Livingston, 50-51
Mark Lohman, 60 (bottom); 62; 94-95; 97; 144 (top)
Michael Lyon, 33 (bottom); 38
Courtesy of Mahan Rykiel Associates Inc., 12 (top)
Rick Mandelkorn, 52
Allan Mandell, 122-123; 141
Joseph W. Molitor, 30
Michael Moran, 98 (top); 99
R. J. Muna, 161 (top right); 171 (bottom); 177 (top right)
John Murdock, 45
Mary E. Nichols, 68-69
Dircum Over, 132
Jeff O'Brien, 65
Peter Paige, 47

Gerald Parker, 154 (bottom)
Erhard Pheiffer, 87 (top)
Courtesy of Pier 1 Imports, 78; 154 (top three)
Anthony Pinto, 74
Undine Pröhl, 40; 133
Marvin Rand, 43
Derek Rath, 130 (top)
Diane Ritch, 174 (top left)
Courtesy of Roche-Bobois, 23
Eric Roth, 6; 9; 13; 21; 35
Larry Scarpa, 110 (bottom)
Russell Shubin, 33 (top)
J. Scott Smith, 54
Eric Staudenmaier, 131
Fred Stocker, 139; 148-149
Tim Street-Porter, 15; 24-25; 36-37; 39 (top); 55; 58; 59; 60 (top); 61; 63; 66; 71; 73; 76 (top); 81 (bottom); 82; 91 (top); 100-101; 103-104; 106-107; 119; 120 (top); 144 (bottom); 152
Studio A/B, 138
Peter Vitale, 96
David Wakeley, 26; 80
Paul Warchol, 86
Alan Weintraub, 57; 114
Charles S. White, 56 (bottom); 102
Vicente Wolf, 129
Mark Woods, 169 (top right)

design credits

Joe Addo, 87 (top)
Michael and Hilary Anderson, 66
Hideaki Ariizumi, 86; 138
David E. Austin, AIA, 83
Barbara Barry, 59; 60 (top); 106 (bottom); 134-135
Hagy Belzberg, 82
Glynis M. Berry, 86; 138
Holly Bieniewski, AIA, 29; 77; 93 (bottom)
James Blakeley, III, ASID, 42
Clelio Boccato, AIA, 27; 92; 130 (top); 133
Peter Q. Bohlin, FAIA, 30-31; 153
Stanley Boles, 88
Gian Franco Brignone, 63
Pamela Burton, 122-123; 125; 141; 148-149
Aviva Bornovski Carmy, 29; 77; 93 (bottom)
Victoria Casasco, 41; 85 (bottom)
David Chemel, 55 (top)
Richard Corsini, 74
Bernard J. Cywinski, FAIA, 30-31; 153
Ilan Dei, 132
Carlos Garcia Delgado, 85 (bottom)
Mayita Dinos, 104
Robin Donaldson, AIA, 84
Tony Duquette, 36-37
Steven Ehrlich, FAIA, 57; 114
Arthur Erickson, 59; 60 (top)
John Erickson, AIA, 55 (top)
James Estes, 56 (top)
Bob Firth, AIA, 27; 92; 130 (top); 133
Ted Flato, 33 (bottom); 38; 39 (bottom); 40
Bernardo Fort-Brescia, FAIA, 76 (top)
Susan Jay Freeman, ASID, 130 (bottom)
Ron Goldman, FAIA, 27; 92; 130 (top); 133
Alexander Gorlin, 28; 46; 53; 81 (top); 98 (top); 99; 150
David Lawrence Gray, FAIA, 24-25; 71; 100-101
David Hacin, 52; 127
Eric Haesloop, 50-51
Julie Hart, 39 (top)
David Hertz, AIA, 44; 87 (bottom); 91; 93 (top)
Charlie Hess, 104
Kim Hoffman, 126
Arata Isozaki, 72
Aleks Istanbullu, 139
Jon C. Jackson, AIA, 30-31; 153
Albert Janz, IIDA, 145
Noel Jeffrey, 96; 151
Sarah Boyer Jenkins, FASID, 98 (bottom); 109
Kevin Johnson, 88
Debbie Jones, 62; 97
Chip Kalleen, IIDA, 128
Annie Kelly, 107 (top)
Christine Kendall-Jent, ASID, IIDA, 58 (top)
Mark D. Kirkhart, AIA, 75
Sandy Koepke, 95
James Kwan, 27; 49
David Lake, 33 (bottom); 38; 39 (bottom); 40
Bill Lane, 56 (bottom); 102
Ricardo Legorreta, 68-70; 124
Donn Logan, 26; 80
Janet Lohman, 94
Mark Mack, 103
Dana Marcu, 83

Lisa Claiborne Matthews, AIA, ASID, 90; 143
Roy McMakin, 55 (bottom); 119
Lee F. Mindel, AIA, 45; 47
Brian Alfred Murphy, 39 (top)
Susan Narduli, AIA, 148-149
David R. Olson, AIA, 65
John O'Neill, 105
Gary Orr, 111-113; 115; 121
Polly Osborne, AIA, 55 (top)
John O'Toole, 88
McKee Patterson, AIA, 32
Michael Palladino, 141
James Palmer, 105
Rob Pressman, ASLA, 110 (top)
Gwynne Pugh, 43; 110 (bottom)
Joseph Ruggiero, 152
Daniel Sachs, 81 (bottom)
Larry Scarpa, 43; 110 (bottom)
Martha Schwartz, 136-137
Josh Schweitzer, 142
Schlesinger & Associates, 24-25
Russell Shubin, AIA, 33 (top); 84
Kathleen Spiegelman, 73; 106 (top)
Laurinda Hope Spear, FAIA, 76 (top)
John Staff, AIA, 54
Odom and Kate Stamps, 107 (bottom)
Timothy Morgan Steele, 33 (top)
Sherry Stein, 145
Rob Steiner, 108
Stephen Suzman, 120 (bottom); 140
Raun Thorp, 58 (bottom); 144 (bottom)
Brian Tichenor, 58 (bottom); 144 (bottom)
Jeffrey Michael Tohl, AIA, 110 (top)
Sallie Trout, 118
Anne Troutman, 64; 76 (bottom); 85 (top)
William Turnbull, Jr., 50-51
Raquel Vert, 131
Diego Villaseñor, 61
Shepard Vineburg, 67
Mark Warwick, 126
Edward Wesely, 98 (bottom); 109
Vicente Wolf, 129
William S. Wolf, 75
Joy Wolfe, ASID, 48
Marcy Li Wong, AIA, 26; 80